The Personal Sphere Model

Raoul A. Schmiedeck, M.D., Ph.D.

Associate Clinical Professor of Psychiatry
Yale University School of Medicine
New Haven, Connecticut

Grune & Stratton

A Subsidiary of Harcourt Brace Jovanovich, Publishers

New York   San Francisco   London

Library of Congress Cataloging in Publication Data

Schmiedeck, Raoul A
  The personal sphere model.

  Bibliography: p.
  1. Projective techniques. 2. Interpersonal
relationships—Testing. I. Title. [DNLM: 1. Projective technics. 2. Interpersonal relations.
3. Object attachment. WM145.3 S354p]
BF698.7.S35   155.2′84   78-9845
ISBN 0-8089-1093-0

Grune & Stratton, Inc.
111 Fifth Avenue
New York, New York 10003

Distributed in the United Kingdom by
Academic Press, Inc. (London) Ltd.
24/28 Oval Road, London NW1

Library of Congress Catalog Number 78-9845
International Standard Book Number 0-8089-1093-0

Printed in the United States of America

Contents

iii

0347214

Acknowledgments

I am grateful to a number of colleagues who have helped me in the work on the *Personal Sphere Model*.

Paul Errera, Lou Micheels, and Gil Rose permitted me to test their patients, and offered advice and comment at various stages. Ernst Prelinger reviewed earlier manuscripts and contributed several basic ideas to the evaluation procedure and the statistical investigation. Th. Kohlmann tested the patients for the project at Vienna University, and helped me in developing some of the measures for the Gestalt of the design. Hans Strotzka made the Vienna project possible and, through continued interest and encouragement, is largely responsible for the publication of this book.

Robert Sollod and Nancy Lyon have worked independently on the *Personal Sphere Model*. Their contributions have been most valuable, and have helped to refine and objectify the test data and to enlarge the area of application.

I am most deeply indebted to Herbert H. Hyman, who helped me in organizing the statistics for this book, and who, through all the phases of my work, has patiently listened to, supported, and, in a most experienced manner, taught me.

R.A.S.

Foreword

Late in 1973, while I was still functioning as editor-in-chief of the *Bulletin of the Menninger Clinic,* I received a promising manuscript from a psychiatrist I remembered as a resident from the Menninger School of Psychiatry. Several things struck me about his paper. First, it discussed a new projective test invented by the author, although it was written by a practicing psychiatrist, a professional breed that does not always appreciate the value of diagnostic testing nor see its ready clinical application. Dr. Schmiedeck took a degree in clinical psychology before he trained as a psychiatrist, and it is undoubtedly this happy combination of clinical and research interests that led him to produce such inventive work at a time when many of our colleagues are proclaiming that psychological testing and perhaps diagnosis itself are moribund.

But that point brings me to the second factor that struck me about Dr. Schmiedeck's early paper. I was impressed that the author was describing not just another test, but a creative application of the projective hypothesis in an area of clinical importance not specifically covered by existing techniques. What this author was proposing was a projective "concretization" of the patient's internal world of objects. With the expansion of the recent interest in object-relations theory, and with developmental research pointing up the crucial significance of early object attachments and the later mental representations of these attachments, it was clear that this paper and the innovative testing efforts it was describing filled a professional need in a new way. I suspect, too, that as has happened to other tests, what is intended as a method for studying object-attachments will end as a method for studying the whole personality. In telling what he thinks about his constellation of relationships, the patient will reveal the large outlines of his functioning self.

Finally, I was surprised that Dr. Schmiedeck was offering his findings to the world for whatever value they could have for the working clinician. He was not attempting to capitalize on the idea for his own material gain, nor was he attempting to erect legal or protective barriers around its use, nor did he find it necessary to call it the Schmiedeck Test. On the contrary, he had become engrossed in a fascinating piece of research, saw its possible utility, was aware of the need it filled, and offered it freely to all who would share his enthusiasm, inviting his colleagues to participate in the experiment and share in its professional rewards.

Needless to say, the editorial board of the *Bulletin of Menninger Clinic* accepted this paper for publication, and now, nearly five years later, Dr. Schmiedeck is returning to his audience with a fully developed test manual that not only describes the test, its administration and scoring, with greater clinical subtlety, but puts it in a context of some developed norms, with standards of interpretation illustrated through a number of case presentations, and its place in clinical research and object-relations theory demonstrated.

Like most ingenious endeavors, the test is a simple idea based on the inference that people have a mental model of their own interpersonal relationships in regard to psychological closeness or distance, negative and positive valences, and dimensions of emotional investment and satisfactions. The test is a way of inviting the patient to make this model explicit, and in such a way that it does not lose its intrinsic complexity or personal significance. My experience with this instrument indicates that most patients are intrigued with the idea of thinking about their relationships in the way suggested by the test, become thoughtful about the drawings they make, and find the test an insight-provoking venture. Sometimes the patients find their drawings surprising, and at other times they discover themselves describing relationships in ways of which they had not been fully conscious.

It is clear that Dr. Schmiedeck has enriched the field of psychological testing with this book, and it is equally clear that those who study and use it are likely to find that it yields information about their patients not easily or systematically gained in any other way.

Sydney Smith, Ph.D.

Formerly, Editor, *Bulletin of the Menninger Clinic,*
Chief Psychologist and Director of Clinical Training for Psychology
The Menninger Foundation

Preface

Personal sphere models are projective tests in which interpersonal relationships are presented by drawings. These drawings are not entirely free, but are guided by instructions which organize and systematize them. In this manner one arrives at designs which can be evaluated impressionistically as well as quantitatively, and offer, as it were, a map of libidinal attachments. From this map conclusions can be drawn about the nature and extent of a person's object relationships.

The initial idea for the test occurred during the planning for a research project on hospitalization in which Paul Errera, Gil Rose, and I collaborated. We felt that individual psychopathology or extraneous circumstances could cause a patient to be hospitalized, but that an additional event, such as the breakdown of a significant relationship, was needed to determine the timing of such a step. It was in the search for a tool that could supplement and confirm the evaluations and observations of a brief period of hospitalization that I conceived of the idea to represent the ties and interruptions of interpersonal relationships graphically. I hoped that such a nonverbal approach would complement and shorten the clinical interviews, and conceivably provide information which was not readily available in verbal contact. From this idea the concept of the personal sphere developed, and eventually the model of the personal sphere.

To begin with, the concept was not rounded, or in any sense complete. Rather, it started out with only a few elements: objects, a "self" in the center of a sphere, connections between this "self" and the objects, and interruptions in the connections. As I experimented with these models, certain groupings and patterns began to appear, norms could be established, and additional test elements and variables were found.

In its present stage, the personal sphere model is sufficiently developed to offer reliable and valid data. It has fulfilled our initial expectations and has proved to be a useful instrument for the assessment of object relationships and for personality research in general. It can be used in conjunction with clinical interviews, as part of a test battery, or independently, and has been found suitable for individual as well as group administration. Nevertheless, the test should still be considered experimental, a project to be pursued, scrutinized, and broadened. In fact, it is one of the attractive features of the test that it frequently seems to offer new vistas and possibilities of combination.

This book is a manual for the personal sphere model, and at the same time an account of its development. It contains instructions, norms, the studies for reliability and validity, examples, and reviews of supporting work. The chapters are so organized that one builds upon the other, and that in reading one can follow the test's growth. Chapter 1 introduces the personal sphere model and the procedures for administration and evaluation, Chapters 2 through 5 describe the variables in detail, and Chapter 6 is devoted to the issues of reliability and validity. In Chapter 7, a series of examples is presented. Chapter 8 contains reports on related and supporting studies, and Chapter 9 reviews the relevant literature and discusses theoretical aspects.

In presenting illustrations, I was faced with a difficult problem of confidentiality. The drawings and the handwriting in personal sphere models, and in particular the names that they contain, give clues to a subject's identity. In most instances these clues will be insufficient for disclosure, but in some rare cases they might conceivably lead to identification. On the other hand, the possibility of changing a model without falsifying the data, and depriving the design of its originality, is quite limited. Since drawings are essential but relatively anonymous, I have left them unchanged. Handwriting is usually limited to single words or short phrases, and often printed rather than put into cursive script—I have therefore left it unchanged, too. But I have covered all names except the most common ones, and have altered all data in clinical descriptions that might compromise a confidence. These precautions would seem to preserve the character of the tests and protect the identities of the subjects.

1

The Basic Test: Description, Administration, and Evaluation*

The original concept of the personal sphere model is based on the idea that the system formed by a person and his relationships can be visualized somewhat along the lines of a molecular model: We assume that each individual stands in the center of a sphere formed by the people, ideas, and things which have influenced him throughout his life and which vary in their importance to him. They may belong to his past or his present, may be closer or farther from him, and his attachments to them may be strong or weak. Some of these relationships may have been highly significant for his development as a person, others only of marginal or temporary importance. One can imagine a person reaching out toward all these objects and, in turn, being dependent on the bonds they extend toward him. In their totality, these objects would form what can be called the Personal Sphere. It would circumscribe the extent of personal relationships, and, if one attempted to represent it graphically, it could be called a model of the personal sphere. In practice, there may be limitations to such a construct, particularly with respect to the dynamic rather than static nature of relationships. Nevertheless, it seems plausible that by following certain instructions, a subject could construct his own personal sphere model and, from this projection, information could be gained about the nature and the extent of his object relationships.

---

* This chapter is a revised and enlarged version of an article by the author published in Bull Menninger Clin 38:113–128, 1974, under the title "The Personal Sphere Model: A New Projective Tool."

In this chapter I shall introduce the test, and describe the administration and evaluation procedures.

The personal sphere model is performed on a white, 11 × 8½-inch card. In the center of the card is a schematically drawn ball, the size of a nickel, printed in black. The subject is told that this ball represents himself; then he is given the following instructions:

Draw around this symbol of yourself, in any way you please, all the people who have been important in your life. If there have been ideas or things of particular importance, include them. Name these objects so that I know who and what they are.

To indicate how important they have been to you, draw from one to three lines between yourself and each object—one line for those of some importance, two for those of moderate importance, and three for those of great importance.

If a relationship has been interrupted, indicate this fact by crossing these connecting lines with one to three crossbars, depending on the degree of the interruption—three crossbars for the most meaningful, two for those of moderate, and one for those of lesser importance.

Frequently it is necessary to add to these instructions that "all the people who have been important in your life" means "those who have been important in the past as well as those who are important in the present." If the subject asks about interruptions and what one means by interruptions, he is told he should decide what would constitute a meaningful interruption to him. Beyond these clarifications, no further guidelines are offered. Routinely, the instructions are given with the same wording and, whenever possible, questions are answered by repeating the identical wording.

The subject decides how he wants to represent his objects, that is, whether he wants to draw them as faces, figures, stick figures, circles, or whatever, how many he wants to draw and how he wants to name them. While no time limit is set for the test, most subjects tend to limit themselves.

What the subject has to work with is a white sheet with a symbol of himself and a set of instructions. Together they form a screen, so to speak, upon which he projects the array of his object relationships. The result is a subjectively drawn map of his libidinal investments.

While the subject works on his model, a *protocol* is kept to record: (1) the *time* it takes to complete the model; (2) the *sequence* in which objects are put down, as well as their *placement* on the sheet, and (3) the *order* in which objects, labels, connecting lines, and crossbars are drawn.

For marking the protocol, I have routinely used O for object, L for label, C for connecting line, and Cr for crossbar. The order in which they are put down may look like this: $O1, L1, C1, Cr1$. Or it may look like this: $O1, O2, O3, C1, C2, C3, Cr3, L1, L2, L3$. Whatever the order or succession, they are marked in the protocol. In addition, notation is made of the subject's hesitations, his corrections, and of his questions and comments. I also include impressions about his mood and reactions, and write down questions I want to ask later.

After the test is completed, usually in 10–20 minutes, the subject is asked to explain any ambiguities. Most often, explanations are needed only to understand some of the labels. The whole test, including the question and answer period, can usually be completed in less than one hour.

EVALUATION

There are two parts to the evaluation. The first part is largely impressionistic and intuitive. It is a kind of first glance, or first summary of one's observations. This part has declined in evaluative importance as the test was further developed, and the number of objective and measurable variables increased. It is still meaningful, though, especially when the measured data alone do not convey a complete picture of the model.

In the second part, the scores, that is, the objective variables, are evaluated one by one.

Impressionistic Evaluation

Just looking at the model, the observer can describe its initial impact on him; the overall organization of the design, the ways or patterns a subject has used to reflect his relationships, and the manner in which he attempts to represent his objects. Seven categories are used to organize these impressions:

GESTALT

This concept refers to the total configuration of the design. Certain Gestalten recur often on the tests and might be considered typical, for example, a wheel or a cluster. There are others which do not occur so frequently, and still others which defy simple description. What should be noted under this heading are the general characteristics of the Gestalt. It may be, for example, confined and cramped or expansive and spreading;

it may be disjointed or it may give a harmonious impression of good balance and good organization.*

FEELING TONE

What feeling does the design convey to the observer? It can be expressed along a continuum between contrasts: alive–dead and friendly–angry. *Alive* would include such attributes as stimulating, interesting, and flexible; *dead* would imply rigid, monotonous, boring, and abstract. *Friendly* would mean nice and pleasant; *angry* would mean aggressive and hostile. One should also be able to sense a degree of comfort or discomfort, and attempt to assess the emotional equilibrium with which a subject maintains his order of object representation. The model can convey a sense of peace, humor, contentment, anxiety, bewilderment, anger, hostility, explosiveness, emptiness, blandness, etc.— in other words, a whole array and mixture of feelings.

USE OF SPACE AND DISTANCE

Again, two pairs of opposites are used to organize one's impressions: full–empty and close–far. *Full–empty* refers to how the space on the sheet has been used. *Close–far* refers to the distances between objects and the "self," and between one object and another. Space may have been used in a complete, encompassing, and inclusive fashion; or it may have been used incompletely, with many areas left uncharted. The objects may all be very far from the "self," or very close to it; or they may be arranged in a mixture.

DEGREE OF DIFFERENTIATION AND SOPHISTICATION

Differentiation includes an assessment of variety versus monotony, and reflects the degree of recognizable grouping and of the use of the same or different drawings for various objects. The degree of sophistication would be assessed along a continuum from primitive to sophisticated. It is a highly impressionistic characteristic and sometimes difficult to gauge. It is related to the complexity of the design, and its intellectual and artistic aspects.

---

* The concept Gestalt will be discussed later, when we come to its measurable aspects. We have found that the Gestalt of a model, especially its "contour"—the outline formed by the objects—changes very little from test to retest. It appears to be a deeply anchored, stable aspect of most personal sphere models.

ORDERLINESS

This characteristic can be assessed along a continuum which moves from orderly to disorderly, or from wild and disturbed to calm and controlled. Obviously, it has to do with the amount of control a subject exerts over his feelings.

OPENNESS

The contrast here lies between open and closed, and reflects the ease of access to the "self." A design can appear tightly closed and guarded, without leaving any space to get through; or it can be open, in either a comfortable or a helpless, unprotected way.

SYMBOLISM

If there is recognizable symbolism, in either the whole design or any of its details, which contributes to an understanding of the subject, it should be noted.

There is, of course, some overlapping of these characteristics, and there will be a tendency to find several related designations for the same model. After seeing a number of personal sphere models, the observer develops a sense for the differences.

Evaluation of Variables

This step is much more objective than the preceding one. There are eleven measurable variables, and six more which are derived from these.

The three basic variables in any model are the objects (O), the connecting lines (C), and the crossbars (Cr).

OBJECTS (O)

In evaluating objects we score their number, nature, and form, along with their placement in space and the sequence in which they were drawn.

Number. Usually one need only to count the objects. Sometimes it is difficult to differentiate whether one, two, or a group of objects are represented, and a judgment has to be made. Most often the number of connecting lines allotted the object or object–complex gives the answer.

Nature.   One must determine whether people, ideas, or things are represented. I have called this factor the *Object-ratio (P-I-Th)*. As will be discussed later, most subjects represent only people *(P-O-O)*, but there still are quite a few who represent people and ideas *(P-I-O)*. Things *(Th)* are rarely included, and if they are, they often stand for ideas.

Form.   Noted here is whether faces, figures, stick figures, circles, etc. are drawn; whether their form is simple or elaborate, careful, or sloppy; whether there is variety; and whether there are signs of disorder and disarray, or of too much control and evenness. At times, it becomes apparent that a relationship to a part object rather than a whole object is being represented.

Placement.   The placement of objects is determined by their location on the clock dial, and their distance from the "self." Location is noted in terms of time; distance is measured in centimeters from the center of the "self" to the nearest point of the object.* Related to the placement of individual objects is the overall manner in which objects are placed into the available space. It may be diffuse, or show clustering or grouping, referring to the relationship of individual objects to each other. It may also be helpful to assess the distance of individual objects from each other. (This category overlaps with the use of space and distance from the impressionistic part of the evaluation, but is more specific.)

Sequence.   The succession in which the objects are drawn during the test is significant and must be recorded in the protocol. This sequence, and the hesitations and alterations that occur in developing it, as well as unexpected choices, can give clues to the relative importance of relationships; for example, when a teacher or therapist is put down first rather than a parent or spouse. An attempt should be made to search for *omissions*. If one has no prior knowledge of the subject, this task may be difficult. Therefore, at the end of the test I usually ask if anybody has been omitted.

CONNECTING LINES *(C)*

The connecting lines are drawn to represent interpersonal relationships, ties, or bonds (I have used these terms interchangeably). Of most

---

* It is helpful to use a transparency with concentric circles 1 cm apart, which can be superimposed on the model. I have also found it useful to mark the placement in the protocol as I follow the subject. In this way, placement and sequence are immediately apparent.

importance are the total number of connecting lines in a model and the number of connecting lines to individual objects, that is, how many objects there are with one, two, or three connecting lines each. It is also helpful to see whether connecting lines touch the "self" or the objects, or whether they enter them or fall short of them. In this sense, one could speak of "complete" or "incomplete" bonds, and of "penetration."

CROSSBARS (Cr)

Again, the total number of crossbars is recorded as well as the number of bars used to cross the connecting lines to individual objects.

INDICES, DISTRIBUTION PATTERNS, AND VALENCES

By combining the three main variables, one arrives at a number of additional variables. The relationship between objects, connecting lines, and crossbars can be expressed in indices. There are two indices for each model:

Bond Index (C/O). This is the index of the ratio of objects to connecting lines. It is called the bond index because it gives us a measure of the "average libidinal investment per object" or, in other words, the "average intensity of relationships." It is computed by dividing the total number of connecting lines by the total number of objects. Its maximum is 3.00, its minimum 0.00 (provided the subject adhered to the instructions).

Separation Index (Cr/C). The separation index, which is the counterpart to the bond index, reflects the ratio of connecting lines to interruptions, and gives us a measure of the "average level of interference" in relationships. To arrive at it, one divides the total number of crossbars by the total number of connecting lines. Its maximum should be 1.00, when tying and separating forces balance each other; its minimum 0.00, when there is no interference whatever (again assuming adherence to the instructions).

The averages of bonding and interfering forces, given in these two measures, are meaningful for the whole model—the totality of relationships in a personal sphere. Additional clues may be gained by establishing similar ratios for individual objects. The individual balance of bonding and interfering forces is called *valence,* and is expressed as the ratio of Cr to C per object (e.g., $2Cr/3C$).

Further clues can be obtained by ordering objects, connecting lines, and crossbars into *distribution patterns,* e.g.,

C	0	1	2	3	more	Total
O	1	2	2	7	—	12

Cr	0	1	2	3	more	Total
O	9	1	2	—	—	12

Distribution patterns are a kind of topical measure. They show how many objects in a given design are strongly and/or weakly cathected, how many more or less intense interruptions there are, and how the intensity of interruptions is related to the strength of the attachments.

MEAN DISTANCE (*MD*) and MEAN DIFFERENCE IN DISTANCE (*MDD*)

The distance for each object is measured from the center of the "self." By dividing the sum of these distances through the number of objects one arrives at the mean distance. The variable *mean distance* is related to the impression "close and far" and the overall size of the Gestalt.

To establish the mean difference in distance we determine how far each object lies from the mean distance (disregarding whether it is closer or farther from the "self"), compute the sum of these smaller distances, and again divide it by the number of objects. The mean difference in distance tells us something about the boundary of the model. For example, if it has a very small value, the objects are obviously kept at very similar distances; that is, the boundary shows little *fluctuation.*

Vollgestalt.   The variable *Vollgestalt* is related to the "full–empty" contrast of the impressionistic part, and is gauged by placing a transparency on the model, which is divided into six sectors. If the model covers all six sectors, it has a "full" Gestalt; if only two or three sectors are covered, it has a "partial" Gestalt. Gestalt is graded from 1 to 6, reflecting the number of covered sectors.

Praegnanz.   The variable *Praegnanz* is borrowed from Gestalt psychology. In order to determine it, we use the results from three other variables: Vollgestalt, mean difference in distance, and form of objects.

The more these three reflect the shape of the "self" (i.e., the ball in the center), the higher we grade for Praegnanz. In other words, a "full" Vollgestalt, low mean difference in distance, and circles for objects, mean very high Praegnanz. Praegnanz is graded from 0 to 6, 0 indicating no Praegnanz, and 6 indicating the highest.

PERCENTAGE OF SYMBOLISMS

This variable is of importance in only a few cases. Symbolisms are relatively rare, and not always clearly recognizable. When they do occur, though, they may have considerable explanatory value and should be noted.

ORDER

Order means the succession of the three basic variables: objects, connecting lines, and crossbars. Labels are a fourth element, although they may stand for the objects themselves.

Since order has been described earlier in this chapter, we must only add that it can be regular or irregular. A succession of $O1, C1, Cr1, L1$, or $O2, C2, L2$, is obviously regular; a succession of $O1, C1$, and $O2, C2, L2$, $Cr1, L1$, is not. Roughly, any order in which elements are added after a delay, during which other objects were started, has to be considered irregular. This includes alterations of an object and its related elements after they were once completed.

All variables listed—in particular, the measures for the number of objects, for connecting lines and crossbars, the indices, and the variables related to Gestalt—permit comparison between different personal sphere models. In the context of statistics and retest studies, I shall discuss these comparisons, the general tendencies of the measures, and their dependency upon one another. At this point, I want to emphasize that the variables differ in importance, and that each one of them represents only a partial aspect of a given test and has to be interrelated.

CASE EXAMPLES

Some individual examples will demonstrate how the test is clinically useful.

Figure 1-1

Example 1-1

This subject was an intelligent, educated woman in her early thirties who had previously gone through a successful analysis. She returned to treatment because of separation problems with her first child. For many years, the patient had suffered from amenorrhea and had been told that she had an organically based endocrine imbalance and could not become pregnant. During and after her analysis, she underwent specialized hormone treatment and began to menstruate regularly. Eventually she became pregnant, but aborted. Some two years later, she became pregnant again, and with a great deal of difficulty was able to carry her child to term.

When she entered her second treatment, she suffered from phobic symptoms and was obsessively concerned with the difficulties of weaning her daughter. She was afraid of harming her, and was unable to give her any freedom. The close, ambivalent, and dependent tie between mother and daughter reflected the kind of relationship the patient had had with *her* mother. Next to this "symbiosis," all other relationships seemed pale. Only in the course of the second treatment could the patient begin to see her husband as a person in his own right and not merely as a dependent and fragile child. The transference was intense and positive and had much to do with another pregnancy that had ended in miscarriage. It was at this time that the personal sphere model (PSM) was administered (see Protocol 1).

SUMMARY OF OBSERVATIONS

After listening to the instructions, the patient paused before starting, smiled, and said, "It is just that I want to make my mother big around me, and that doesn't fit." Then she drew (Fig. 1-1) her mother ($O1$) as the first object, then her father ($O2$) right next to her mother. She waited a bit, drew her husband ($O3$), then erased and redrew him. While these three objects had been put quite close to the center, the next object ($O4$)—which turned out to be me (therapist)—was placed a little farther away. After a pause, she drew her sister ($O5$) rather slowly and carefully and also placed her farther away. After another pause, she then drew her daughter ($O6$), drawn very close, touching her. Again, she erased and redrew. Then came the miscarriage ($O7$) and, after a pause, a teacher and friend ($O8$). This face, too, she erased and then enlarged. A former boyfriend ($O9$) followed and then to the left of him, the patient's previous therapist ($O10$). After another pause came the eleventh object ($O11$), all the way at the bottom of the page.

Up to this point, the patient had not drawn a single connecting line, nor had she labeled any of the objects. Now she provided the labels—first her former therapist, then my initials, then father, mother, teacher, husband, sister, daughter, the miscarriage, and finally the label for object 11, which turned out to be a little boy whom her mother had taken in as a foster child when the patient was very young. She explained more about him later. At this point, she added object 12, another little boy who also was a foster child in her family. She was about to stop, when she suddenly remembered: "I forgot the lines." She put them down in the following sequence: father, mother, husband, myself (therapist), sister, miscarriage, teacher, boyfriend, former therapist, the two little boys. In this she followed the sequence in which she originally put down her objects, except for reversing her parents.

The subject took about ten minutes to complete the PSM. The rest of the hour was spent in voluntarily explaining her answers and responding to questions.

EVALUATION (INCLUDING QUESTIONS & ANSWERS)

Taking first the impressionistic part of the evaluation, the design appears to be alive but not very full. It is orderly, friendly, open, and rather sophisticated. Objects are both close and far from the center, that is, the "self." Also, the design is differentiated, clearly showing groupings of objects.

There are twelve objects, all people, including a miscarriage (which is

Protocol 1-1

Order & Sequence (O,C,Cr,L)	Object[a]	Placement Distance[a]	Location
O1	Mother	3	1
O2	Father	2	12
O3	Husband	2	8
O4	Therapist	5	10
O5	Sister	6	3
O6	Child	0	4
O7	Miscarriage	8	4
O8	Teacher/Friend	10	1
O9	Former boyfriend	12	11
O10	Former therapist	13	11
O11	Little boy	12	5
L10,L9,L4,L2,L1,L8,L3, L5,L6,L7,L11			
O12,L12	Little boy	12	5

C2(3), C1(3), C3(3), C4(3), C5(3), C7(1), C8(1), C9(3), C10(3), C12(2), C11(2)

Omissions: female cousin

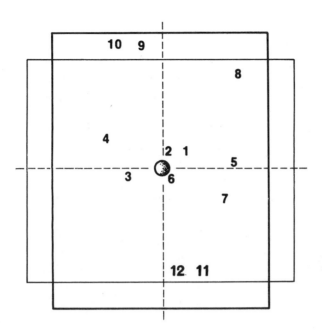

Valence[a] (Cr/C)	Comments	Remarks & Observations
O/3	It's just that I want to make my mother big."	waits, smiles. . .
O/3		
O/3		erases, redraws
O/3		No C or L so far
O/3		carefully drawn
?		erases, redraws
O/1		does not talk
O/1		erases, enlarges O
O/3		God?, at 12 o'clock
O/3		
O/2		Still no C or L. Now!
O/2	"I guess that's it. Oh, I forgot the lines!"	Forgot instructions

Time: 10 minutes

[a] Filled in after completion of test.

Scoring Sheet 1-1
Time: 10 minutes

A. Impressions

---

1. *Gestalt*   partial, but expansive, groupings, organized
2. *Feeling tone*
   (alive–dead; friendly–angry)   rather alive; friendly
3. *Space & Distance*
   (full–empty; close–far)   neither full nor empty
4. *Differentiation and Sophistication*
   (primitive–sophisticated)   sophisticated
5. *Orderliness*
   (orderly–disorderly; calm–wild)   fairly orderly
6. *Openness* (open–closed)   fairly open
7. *Symbolisms*   miscarriage, wavy and broken lines

B. Variables

---

1. *Objects*
   Number   12
   Nature (P/I/Th)   11/1/0   I%
   Form   Faces
   Placement   Clustering
   Sequence   Mother, father, husband, therapist, sister, child, miscarriage, teacher, boyfriend, former therapist, two little boys
2. *Connecting lines (C)*   27, some "broken," one to miscarriage "penetrates"
3. *Crossbars (Cr)*   0
4. *Bond Index (C/O)*   2.25 (27/12)
5. *Separation Index (Cr/C)*   0.0, cannot be established
6. *Valences*   see Protocol 1
7. *Distribution patterns*

C	0	1	2	3	more	Total
O	1	2	2	7	—	12

Cr	0	1	2	3	more	Total
O	12	—	—	—	—	12

8. *Mean Distance (MD)*   7.1
9. *Mean Difference in Dist. (MDD)*   4.2
10. *Vollgestalt*   4
11. *Praegnanz*   2

| 12. | *Percent of Symbolisms* | about 10%, difficult to assess |
| 13. | *Order* | irregular, compartmentalized, first all *O*, then all *L*, then all *C*. No *Cr*. |

counted as an "idea" on the scoring sheet, but could be seen as either). A closer look reveals that there are really two miscarriages, both connected with the same tie: a wavy line which, without too much imagination, can be seen as an umbilical cord. All objects are represented as faces.

We turn at this point to some of the test characteristics. One can see evidence of grouping or clustering. Distance is used not only to indicate distance in time, but also to show the degree of involvement. Children are placed below the horizon, adults above; yet, her husband is placed slightly below. Women are put to the right, men (except her father) to the left, and, of course, her daughter touches her. The daughter is the only object to whom she did not draw a connecting line; that would have been impossible because of the closeness. The patient drew a total of 27 connecting lines. There are seven objects with three connecting lines each, two with two, and two with one.

But the patient "misunderstood" the instructions and did not draw crossbars. Instead, she drew broken lines. In the narrower sense of the instructions, these broken lines cannot be evaluated; that is, one is not able to establish a separation index (*Cr/C*). This result reveals the difficulty the patient has in indicating and conceptualizing separations. Much of what the patient has drawn is self-explanatory. Some of her comments, however, are very informative.

She explained that object 8 was the director of education at her college. They became friends later when the patient married. "This woman considers herself a mother to me. I like her, but I think she neglects me." Object 12 is "a little boy mother took care of. He ended in a home for the feebleminded. My parents never forgave themselves. He was with us from infancy to about age three. I was close in age to him."

Of object 11 she said: "We got him when he was four months old and kept him until the age of six years, when he went into a home for disturbed children. I went to college then. This one was schizophrenic. My parents also feel very guilty over him."

Object 9 is her boyfriend: "He was a great love when I was sixteen. He went out with my sister and then took me out for four years. The only one I ever loved besides my husband. After he broke with me, I didn't love anybody for years."

When I asked the patient why she drew no crossbars, she said, "I drew broken lines. The wavy line was my idea." The area below the horizon, she felt, represented the unconscious: "Things down there are still bothering me." Up or above the horizon, the objects were in her memory but not very painfully. Why had she drawn faces? "I was terribly afraid of doing bodies. I did not want to draw my own or other bodies. I drew people a little bit as I see them. This will tell you more."

The patient omitted one object, a female cousin considerably older than herself who is a career woman and whom she dislikes.

The bond index can be established, although not convincingly because of her use of broken lines. It is 2.25, which would indicate a good or better than "average intensity of relationships."

CONCLUSION

This subject has strong and also strongly ambivalent relationships. They are only few, in the present as well as the past, but appear to be meaningful and well remembered. Her main difficulty centers around separations. It is severe, to the point of making her "break rules"; that is, she forgot or disregarded the instructions. However, she remained well organized and even became intentive. She tends to compartmentalize and, at the present time at least, appears constricted. (See the closeness of every object in her present. The impression of expansiveness is misleading, the "far" objects all belong to the past.) The relationships to her daughter is obviously at the core of her conflict.

Example 1-2

This subject was a middle-aged woman whose second marriage was about to fall apart. Her first marriage had ended in divorce and, even though the present one had not been good either, she saw its end as a symbol of personal failure and final rejection. Her sense of self-worth was shaken; her pride in being an intelligent, self-sufficient woman had given way to despair and self-accusation, alternating with furious rages against her present husband, whom she held responsible for her fate. There were some involutional elements and signs of a deeper disturbance of object relationships and of isolation underneath a facade of hysterical, agitated behavior.

The patient had left her native England shortly after World War II, and since then had only minimal contact with her original family. She had two adolescent children from her first marriage and a small son from her second.

SUMMARY OF OBSERVATIONS

The patient began (See Fig. 1-2 and Protocol 2) with her youngest child ($O1$), followed by the next in age, a daughter ($O2$), and the oldest, a

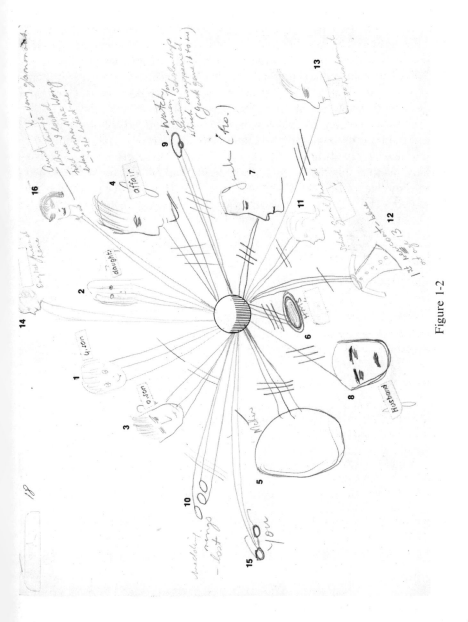

Figure 1-2

son (*O3*). As she drew the faces, she immediately drew connecting lines and wrote labels. A closer look at these three faces shows that her youngest son looks rather friendly and sheepish. Next came a man (*O4*) with whom the patient had had a long-lasting affair between her two marriages. She drew him big with heavy lines, and then crossed the ties to him three times. After a moment's hesitation, she added crossbars to her two sons and drew her daughter's hair a little longer. To me she said, "This is really just who is important to me, isn't it?" After a while, crying now, she said, "I just cannot draw my mother—that is silly." She then proceeded to draw her mother (*O5*) as a big blob, which she placed in opposition to her boyfriend. Again, she quickly added three crossbars. Next, almost doodling, she drew another hard-to-recognize symbol (*O6*) which also received three connecting lines and three crossbars. Later it turned out that this figure was the ship she had served on in the Royal Navy. She had joined the Navy in World War II at the age of 18 in what appeared to be a legitimized method of running away from home. Next, the patient went back and redrew the crossbars over the ties to her

Protocol 1-2

Order & Sequence (*O,C,Cr,L*)	Object[a]	Placement Distance[a]	Location
$O1,C1(3),L1$	Young son	6	11
$O2,C2(3),L2$	Daughter	5	12
$O3,C3(3),L3$	Older son	5	10
$O4,C4(3),L4,Cr1(1),Cr3(2)$	Affair	6	2
$O5,C5(3),L5,Cr5(2)$	Mother	6	8
$O6,C6(3),L6,Cr6(3)$	Ship	2.5	6
$O7,C7(2),L7,Cr7(3)$	Older brother	5	3
$O8,C8(1),L8,Cr8(3)$	Husband	6	7
$O9,C9(3),L9,Cr9(3)$	Watch	8	2
$O10,C10(3),L10,Cr10(3)$	Rings	8.5	10
$O11,L11,C11(2),Cr11(2)$	Former girlfriend	5	5
$O12,C12(3),L12,Cr12(1)$	Coat	6	6
$C13(1),O13,L13,Cr13(3)$	1st husb.	11	4
$C14(2),O14,L14$	Present girlfriend	10	12
$O15,C15(2),L15,Cr15(1)$	Therapist	11	9
$O16,L16,C16(2)$	Aunt	9	1

Omissions: Father, 6 siblings

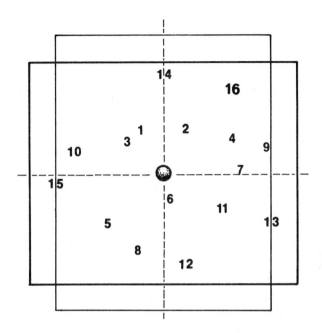

Valence[a] (Cr/C)	Comments	Remarks & Observations
1/3		
0/3		
2/3	"My hand shakes"	lights cigarette
3/3		very big, heavy
3/3	"This is really . . . I cannot."	draws daughter's hair longer, Sy,[b] cries!
3/3		Sy, redraws Cr5
3/2		
3/1	"They are all men"	big, emph. eyes, outlines jaw, Sy, erases, adds,
3/3		
3/3	"This is all my life?"	
2/2		waits
1/3	"The first new thing . . ."	erases, redraws
3/1		waits, looks for space
0/2		cigarette, waits
1/2	"The parallel lines . . . I mean the crossbars are separations?"	Sy
0/2		

Time: 35 minutes

[a] Filled in after completion of test.

[b] Symbolism.

mother. Then she drew her brother Jack (*O*7), her oldest sibling, her mother's favorite, and a father substitute. The patient's father had been a vague, distant figure. He is omitted from the design, as are her other six siblings.

Object 8 is the patient's present husband, drawn as a mask, with heavy emphasis on the eyes and mouth, and placed in close proximity to her mother and the ship. As she went on, the patient emphasized the crossbars and said: "They are all men" (although she had just placed the greatest emphasis on the crossbars to her mother!).

Object 9 is a watch given her by her brother Jack for "scholarship," which she later lost. Once more she returned to the ties to mother and their interruptions. Then she drew her wedding rings (*O*10), three of them, then a girlfriend from school (*O*11). After a long wait and a remark, "This is ally my life? Right?" the patient continued. She drew and redrew object 12, a coat, "The first new thing I ever got from my mother," and "Mother gave it away later."

The patient's first husband (*O*13) was next. There is only one tie to him, but there are three crossbars. She went on to object 14, an English woman friend in her present life. Object 15 is a pair of glasses, which represents me, and object 16 is an aunt who liked the patient and is described as glamorous.

Scoring Sheet 1-2
Time: 35 minutes

A.	Impressions	
1.	*Gestalt*	explosive, disorganized, uneven
2.	*Feeling tone* (alive–dead; friendly–angry)	alive; angry
3.	*Space and Distance* (full–empty; close–far)	full; nothing very close, rather far
4.	*Differentiation and Sophistication* (primitive–sophisticated)	differentiated, but questionable grouping, sophisticated and primitive elements
5.	*Orderliness* (orderly–disorderly; calm–wild	rather disorderly and wild
6.	*Openness* (open–closed)	rather closed
7.	*Sybolisms*	Mother, husband, therapist, ship

B.	Variables	
1.	*Objects* Number	16
	Nature (P/I/Th)	12/0/4, all 4 *Th* stand for Ideas

Form		Faces and drawings
Placement		scattered, somewhat confused, some grouping
Sequence		Young son, daughter, older son, man (affair), mother, ship, older brother, husband, watch, wedding rings, former girlfriend, coat, first husband, present girlfriend, therapist, aunt
2.	*Connecting lines (C)*	39
3.	*Crossbars (Cr)*	31
4.	*Bond Index (C/O)*	2.44 (39/16) rather high
5.	*Separation Index (Cr/C)*	0.79 (31/39) high
6.	*Valences*	see Protocol 2
7.	*Distribution patterns*	

C	0	1	2	3	more	Total
O	0	2	5	9	—	16

Cr	0	1	2	3	more	Total
O	3[a]	3	2	8	—	16

8.	*Mean Distance (MD)*	6.9
9.	*Mean Difference in Distance (MDD)*	1.9 (about 1/4 MD)
10.	*Vollgestalt*	6
11.	*Praegnanz*	2
12.	*Percent of Symbolisms*	25%, high
13.	*Order*	really quite regular with slight variations. One definite irregularity (*Cr* for the two sons).

[a] All around 12 o'clock; all female.

EVALUATION (INCLUDING QUESTIONS AND ANSWERS)

From an impressionistic standpoint, the design is alive and full, looking rather wild and disorganized. It is differentiated, but the grouping of objects remains indistinct, except possibly for her children, who are in one area (objects 1–3). The objects fall between being close and far, but none is very close. The design is angry but not altogether unfriendly, and one senses that the anger is explosive. There are both sophisticated and primitive elements. The overall impression is one of confusion, centrifugal forces, mixing of concepts, and a lack or failure of structure.

There are 16 objects: nine faces, obviously representing people, and seven other objects, three of which also represent people. The four remaining objects (things) really represent ideas, that is, memories and experiences. Balancing somewhat the impression of confusion and disarray, the objects are fairly well defined in their form, show considerable variety, and seem to be well conceived.

There is a total of 39 connecting lines, with 16 objects. Thus, the bond index is 2.44. There are 31 crossbars, with half the patient's object relationships carrying these crossbars. All grown men and her mother belong to this group. The separation index is 0.79, which is high.

The patient's father is omitted, and the therapist depersonalized. There is only one person with three connecting lines without crossbars— the patient's daughter. Even her two sons carry crossbars. There can be no doubt about the serious disturbance in object relationships and the intensity with which she experiences separations. There are three indications—such as the mask representing her husband, the blob which she calls mother, and the glasses standing for me—that some of her relationships are to part, rather than whole, objects.

CONCLUSION

The subject's relationships are highly ambivalent, marked by intense attachment and equally intense rage. There are signs that she easily regresses to a level of primitive (oral) object relationships, and can hardly contain the conflict between dependency and disappointment. She manages it by taking recourse to a good sense for form (faces, drawings), and to compulsive defenses which still hold (order).

Example 1-3

While the two preceding models are alive and interesting, the following example seems dead and unimaginative.

It is the work of a 26-year-old former monk who entered treatment because of a vague sense of emptiness and depression. He was the youngest of three children born into a lower-middle-class family, but grew up like an only child because his siblings were much older. His father was a distant man who died when the patient was in his late teens. His mother was once very close to him—she was largely responsible for his religious upbringing—but now also seemed remote. The patient did well in high school, went to college, but soon found himself in doubt about career goals and, at the age of 20, entered a monastery. After several years in the monastery, he could no longer accept the discipline and developed difficulties in concentration. Eventually he was asked to leave, with the recommendation to seek treatment. By the time he came to see me, he had reentered college and worked in an office. He was lonely, depressed, angry at the monastery and his religion, and unable to make friends.

SUMMARY OF OBSERVATIONS

The subject worked silently and without showing emotions (see Protocol 3). The first four objects (see Fig. 1-3) represent areas of immediate concern. School ($O1$) is of paramount importance. He wants to finish but is worried that he might not be able to study. Work ($O3$) provides his living, but he is not sure of his competence. He lives with a brother ($O2$)

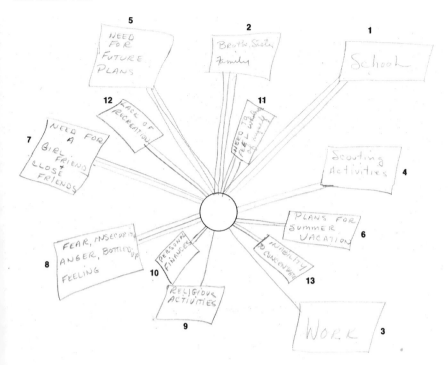

Figure 1-3. In the early stages of experimentation with the PSM, the subjects were given the choice of two representations of the "self": the schematically drawn ball, or an empty circle. This subject selected the circle.

and the brother's family; but he seems to mean his *original* family. Into this box (O2), he has crowded all direct human contact. There are no other "people" in the test. Scouting activities (O4) are part of his past, but also his only recreational activity in the present.

All the other objects are really thoughts, providing us with a list of his concerns, needs, and fears. If we go by valences (connecting lines, that is, in his case), he tells us that he is very anxious about his future, urgently needs a girl friend, or friends in general, and that he is anxious about the anger inside him and his inability to feel whole. Each of these "ideas" carries 3 C (O5, O7, O8 and O11).

The subject's further concerns seem to flow from these four, but may be more immediate—they are, in fact, placed closer to the "self": Plans for the summer (O6), worries about finances (O10), about relaxation, something to do when he does not work (O12), and about difficulties in concentration (O13). They carry two connecting lines each. The one connecting line for religious activities (O9) looks suspicious—one would expect stronger investment. But it may be correct if he means his limited religious involvement of the present, and not the deeper conflict. Important also are the omissions, and the fact that he did not draw one single crossbar.

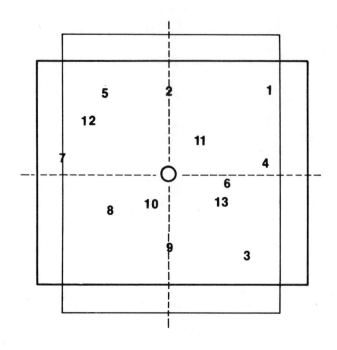

Protocol 1-3

Order & Sequence (O,C,Cr,L)	Object[a]	Placement Distance[a]	Location
O1,L1,C1(3)	School	9	1
O2,L2,C2(3)	Family	7	12
O3,L3,C3(1)	Work	6	5
O4,L4,C4(2)	Scouting	5	2
O5,L5,C5(3)	Future plans	7	11
C6(2),O6,L6	Summer plans	3.5	3
C7(3),O7,L7	Need girlfriend	6.5	10
C8(3),O8,L8	Fear	4	8
C9(1),O9,L9	Religion	3.5	6
C10(2),O10,L10	Finances	2	7
C11(3),O11,L11	Need to feel myself	2.5	12
C12(2),O12,L12	Lack of recreation	5	10
C13(2),O13,L13	Inability to concentrate	2.5	4

Omissions: Father, Mother, unless included under family. Priests from monastery, Therapist?

[a] Filled in after completion of test.

Scoring Sheet 1-3
Time: 15 minutes

A.	Impressions	
1.	*Gestalt*	simple, two concentric "wheels" of Labels and boxes.
2.	*Feeling tone* (alive–dead; friendly–angry	monotonous, bland, mechanical
3.	*Space and Distance* (full–empty; close–far)	nothing really close or far
4.	*Differentiation and Sophistication* (primitive–sophisticated)	unsophisticated and undifferentiated, quite compulsive and compartmentalized
5.	*Orderliness* (orderly–disorderly; calm–wild)	orderly; too calm
6.	*Openness* (open–closed)	not open and not closed
7.	*Symbolisms*	none, unless we count the boxes as symbolic

Valence[a] (*Cr/C*)	Comments	Remarks & Observations
0/3		waits, begins, waits
0/3		
0/1		
0/2	"Can it be something not concrete?"	erases 1C to O4
0/3		
0/2		
0/3		erases, adds to O7
0/3		
0/1		erases, rewrites O9
0/2		erases, enlarges O5
0/3		silent, serious
0/2		
0/2		

Time: 15 minutes

B.   Variables

---

1.   *Objects*
     Number   13
     Nature (P/I/Th)   1/12/0 many ideas, too many!
     Form   "Labels only," in boxes
     Placement   concentric, even arrangement,
                                       possibly some clustering
     Sequence   School, family, work, scouting, future
                                       plans, summer plans, need for girlfriend,
                                       fears, etc., religious activity,
                                       wholeness of self, need for recreation,
                                       difficulty in concentration
2.   *Connecting lines (C)*   30
3.   *Crossbars (Cr)*   0
4.   *Bond Index (C/O)*   2.3 (30/13)
5.   *Separation Index (Cr/C)*   0.0
6.   *Valences*   see protocol
7.   *Distribution patterns*

C	0	1	2	3	more	Total
O	0	2	5	6	—	13

Cr	0	1	2	3	more	Total
O	13	—	—	—	—	13

8.   *Mean Distance (MD)*   5.0
9.   *Mean Difference in Distance*
     (MDD)   1.6 (about 1/3MD)
10. *Vollgestalt*   6
11. *Praegnanz*   3
12. *Percent of Symbolisms*   0
13. *Order*   very regular, one slight variation

EVALUATION (INCLUDING QUESTIONS AND
ANSWERS)

   Impressionistically, this is an empty, unemotional design, which
looks like an arrangement of placards. It is orderly, but not impressively
so. The boxes support the sense of order, but also a sense of intellectuali-
zation and isolation. One has to put effort into this model in order to
extract information.

   The number of objects (13) lies within the normal range, but only one
object represents "people"—all others are "ideas." This is significant. It
speaks for severe impoverishment of object relationships, withdrawal
from the world, and preoccupation with narcissistic concerns. That this
withdrawal is not total, though, and may not be too severe, can be gleaned

from the content of several ideas. They are concerned with activities in which other people are involved.

Some clues as to the subject's conflicts are given through sequence and clustering. It appears that the fear of his "bottled up anger" is related to "religious activities," and that his insecurity may be connected with financial worries, that is, the loss of the security he must have had in the monastery (O8, O9, and O10 in the lower left quadrant). Similarly, there seems to be a connection between the "lack of recreation," his "need for a girlfriend . . . ," and his concern about the future (O12, O7, and O5). Some meaning might be read into the arrangement in two concentric circles. The inner circle deals with more immediate, present issues, while the outer one contains concerns of a general nature which extend into the past as well as the future.

The bond index of 2.3, together with the missing separation index, should be interpreted as in *Example 1*, as an expression of intense dependency needs. The distribution pattern for connecting lines shows fewer objects with 3C each than we found in the corresponding patterns of the two preceding examples. This finding is impressive when one considers that this subject's bonds are not to people, but to his own thoughts.

The findings for Vollgestalt, Praegnanz, and Order speak for a good deal of conventionalism and compulsivity. He is clearly not inventive or sophisticated. Rather, he seems, at least at the present, constricted, plodding, and laboring under conflict.

Some remarks from the question and answer period are very informative:

When I asked why there were so few people in his model he said, "I have a lack of people . . . I think that's my whole problem." And when I inquired about his parents, "Well, my father is dead, so he is out of the picture. . . . As far as good things are concerned, mother is out of the picture, too. She is not the same person I remember."

CONCLUSION

This subject has withdrawn from object relationships. It is likely that they were always limited, and marked by dependency and the need for nurture. He is deeply conflicted, isolated, depressed, and suspicious. But his conflicts seem to have little emotional resonance. He is almost flat, and his depression is experienced mostly as emptiness. The subject has some well-functioning compulsive defenses (in work, mostly), and appears to be an intellectualizer. The impoverishment of object relationships, combined with the concentration on narcissistic ideas, speaks for borderline psychosis, probably borderline schizophrenia.

With these examples I have concluded the introduction to the personal sphere model. In the following four chapters the test variables will be described in greater detail, and further defined and discussed.

2
Test Variables: Objects

The description of the variables and elements of the personal sphere model follows the order in which they are usually placed in the test. Incidentally, this sequence also happens to show how the test developed. Statistical norms are presented separately for each variable, and again in summary form in Chapter 5.

The sample, on which the statistics are based, consisted of 136 subjects, all lower- to upper-middle-class white Americans. Of these subjects, 80 were female and 56 were male; 86 were married, 31 were single, and 19 were divorced or separated. There were 27 adolescents or young adults in the sample, ranging in age from 14 to 22, and 109 adults, mostly in their thirties and forties.

All the subjects were in out-patient psychotherapy at the time they took the test, except for seven who were hospitalized. They presented a wide range of clinical conditions, from transient situational reactions to severe psychotic impairment. In most cases, though, the clinical picture remained well within neurotic proportions.

CHARACTERISTICS

One can distinguish five separate characteristics for objects: their number, nature, form, placement and sequence.

Number

The interquartile range (see Table 2-1) lies between 10 and 20 objects, for "people only" between 8 and 18. From this area of greatest density the field thins out, mostly upwards. Models containing fewer than seven or more than 26 objects are rare.

In developing his design, a subject seems to go through stages. At first, "significant people" (i.e., members of the original or present families, and maybe one or two others, such as a therapist or a mentor) are drawn. I have called this the subsphere No. 1. Depending on the size of the families, the number of objects will vary from about seven to 12. Beyond this original subsphere, thinking begins. That is, one has to think now whom one will include. A second set is being developed, a subsphere of people who have been friends, lovers, influential teachers, and the like. Ideas and goals of value are included at this stage. The number of objects will reach 14, 15, or perhaps 18. Most subjects stop here if they have not stopped after the first set. If a subject goes on, he seems to be "filling-in" rather than adding meaningful relationships.

"Filling-in" does not begin right after 18 objects, but certainly after 20–22. I have seen "filling-in" mostly in obsessive–compulsive characters, or in those who are suspicious and paranoid. It may mean that these subjects wish to show that they have many important relationships in order to hide how few there really are; or, they may, after having completed the first set, which is sort of traditional and obligatory, find themselves unable to differentiate who is important and who not. Their libidinal investments are tenuous, and, for safety's sake, they keep adding objects.

The number of objects is a very stable variable. In the test–retest study we found that its mean remained the same, and that there were also few intraindividual changes. In other words, the number of objects a subject places in his test appears to be consistent and more or less typical. Individual objects may be exchanged, but these shifts are minor, and even long intervals between tests or intervening treatments seem to have little influence on the number of objects which are considered "important."

Table 2-1
Number of Objects ($N = 136$)

	All Objects	People Only
Range	6–43	1–40
$Q1$	10	8–9
Median	14	12
$Q3$	20	17–18

Nature

We differentiate "people" (*P*), "ideas" (*I*), and "things" (*Th*), among the objects in personal sphere models, and record their relative frequency in the *object-ratio (P/I/Th)*.

"People" are by far the most important kind of object. They are represented in every test and usually constitute the majority of objects. About 50% of the models in our sample contained "people only" *(P/O/O)*. In rare cases, the number of "people" was small—2, 3, or 4. In most instances it ranged between 8 and 18. We had no case without "people."

Once in a while we found animals in personal sphere models, usually dogs or cats. We have counted these animals as "people" because it seemed that they represented displacements from the subject himself (adolescents), or from children and pregnancies (women).

"Ideas" are not in every test. We found them in half of the sample, and usually only one or two in a test. The tendency to include "ideas" was greatest among men and the young. Also, if there were "ideas" in a test, their frequency tended to increase with the number of objects. Up to 12 objects, we found about 10% "ideas"; up to 20 objects about 25%, and in tests with more than 25 objects, 30% "ideas."

The "ideas" in a test can have a host of meanings. They can stand for experiences and memories, phases in life, aspirations, beliefs, philosophies, occupations, and preoccupations. It is impossible to offer a complete list. However, we found that the *percentage of ideas* in individual models has diagnostic meaning. It appears that one should think of more than three "ideas" as *many ideas*. When the percentage of ideas approaches 30%, this indicates a preoccupation with issues which are narcissistically cathected and have to do with the "self" and its orientation in the world. Subjects with more than 50% "ideas" were psychotic or borderline psychotic.

"Things" are seldom found in personal sphere models. Before we go into detail, we should discuss the difference between "things" and "ideas."

"Ideas" are either written on the sheet—as words or phrases, such as "religion," or "my career"—or they are pictured as drawings; for example, books standing for an interest in reading, a house representing the home where one grew up, or a scale indicating a concern with justice. Since "things" are also represented as drawings, it may become difficult to distinguish whether the subject meant the "idea" or the material "thing." Also, many "things" stand for ideas. When an adolescent, for example, draws a car, or a guitar, these "things" do not only mean the material thing, but are also symbols for independence, or virility, or the sense of belonging to a subculture. In most instances, one can clarify the issue by asking.

There is, of course, the question of how important such a differentiation is. After working with the test for some time, it seemed quite artificial to me. I dropped the designation "things" and retained only "people" and "ideas."

Later on, however, as more data were accumulated, it became advisable to reintroduce them. "Things" are rare, and found almost exclusively in the models of adolescents, but they do occur—as material things—and seem to have a meaning of their own. Sollod (1977), who used the personal sphere model to examine over 300 college students, reports a significant positive correlation between the number of "things" and the number of crossbars in their models, particularly the number of crossbars assigned to members of their families. No such correlation existed between crossbars and the number of "ideas." The meaning of this finding is not clear. Apparently it has to do with the age of the subjects, which is one of separation from their families. One might speculate that the "things" in their models represent transitional objects.

We have to return briefly to "ideas." As mentioned above, the "percentage of ideas" increases with the number of objects. Models with over 30% "ideas" often have a third subsphere, where objects are "filled in." One may have to differentiate, therefore, between "filling in" with "people," which we discussed earlier, and "filling in" with "ideas," which appears to be indicative of a preoccupation with self-centered issues and conflicts.

In an investigation of self and nonself regions, Prelinger (1959) ranked certain concepts according to the degree to which they were perceived to be part of the self (the "mine" sphere). Clearly considered part of the self were body parts, psychological and intraorganismic processes, personal identifying characteristics, intimate possessions, and physiological productions. Closest in the nonself region were abstract ideas.

The "ideas" in the personal sphere model almost always carry a high emotional charge and are apparently considered part of the self, or at least as close to the self as "people." In contrast to "people," however, they are more easily exchanged or left out on retests. The "percentage of ideas" is one of the less stable variables, and intra-individual fluctuations in the number of ideas are fairly frequent.

Form

There are four forms of objects: labels, circles, stick figures, and faces and figures. Circles are the most frequently used form. Together with occasional squares and rectangles, they were drawn by 40% of the subjects. Slightly more than 25% of the subjects used stick figures, and slightly less than 25% only labels (without any drawings). Ten percent of the subjects drew faces and figures. In some instances, faces and figures were mixed with other forms.

Placement

The placement of objects proved to be one of the more interesting and intriguing aspects of the personal sphere model. The attempt to investigate it, however, met with built-in limitations. The models contain so many different and varied objects that it is impossible to fit them all into a system from which generally applicable trends can be deduced. We decided to concentrate our examination on objects (or, more correctly, "people") with whom everybody has a special relationship, and who can therefore be expected to show up in every test, and in sufficient numbers. These objects are the so-called "significant people, that is, parents, grandparents, siblings, spouses, children, and sexual partners (other than spouses). To this list we added the therapists and the dead.

To pinpoint placement, we used the *location* of an object on the clockface, and its *distance* from the "self." The latter we expressed as a percentage of each model's mean distance, in order to make it comparable.* The resulting areas of *preferred placement* represent those sectors on the clockface in which we found 50% of the members of each category of "significant people." We checked these areas for significance through chi-square against a random distribution, and against the base distribution for all "significant people" ($N = 982$).

Against a random distribution, all preferred placement areas were significant on the level of 0.01; against the base distribution of all "significant people" we found differences in placement for parents, children, and sexual partners (on the level of 0.01), and for the dead (on the level of 0.05).

Figure 2-1 shows the base distribution for all "significant people."

This base distribution indicates bunching in the upper half, in particular in the upper right quadrant. The question remains whether a base including all objects, not only "significant people," would show a similar

---

* The actual distance in centimeters, as it is normally measured, would have been useless. It permits comparison only between the distances of objects in one model. In order to adapt these measures for our purposes, we expressed the distance for each "significant object" as a percentage of the model's mean distance (e.g., mother at 85% MD, grandfather at 110% MD). We then computed the means of these percentages for all models, and in this way obtained a "standard" distance for each category (e.g., parents = 87%, grandparents = 108%).

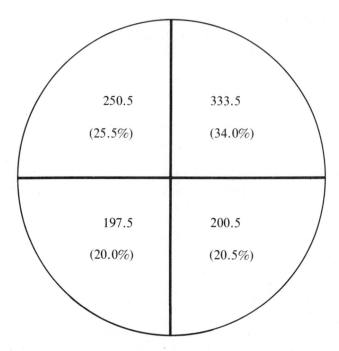

Figure 2-1.   Base distribution for all "significant people." ($N = 982$).

pattern. I have not been able to check it, but I assume it would. "Significant people" provide the bulk of the objects in tests which are limited to subspheres nos. 1 and 2, and most tests in our sample are of this kind. Also, there seems to be a cultural preference for the upper half and the upper right quadrant in anything we write or draw. Pecjak (1972) investigated Yugoslav and Zambian subjects with a form of the graphic semantic differential, and found significant differences in the spatial locations that these two groups assigned to affectively charged terms. Words such as "friend–enemy" and "goodness–evil" were arranged along the dimension center–periphery by both the Zambians and the Yugoslavs. However, the Yugoslavs also arranged them along the dimensions above–below (a horizontal division), and left–right (a vertical division). According to Pecjak, the dimension center–periphery has universal character, while the dimensions above–below and left–right have their origin in European culture.

From the base distribution, we would expect to find relatively more objects in the upper half and the upper right quadrant of a model. The actual distribution of "significant people," their *areas of preferred placement*, is listed in Table 2-2, and graphically represented in Figure 2-2.

Areas of preferred placement.

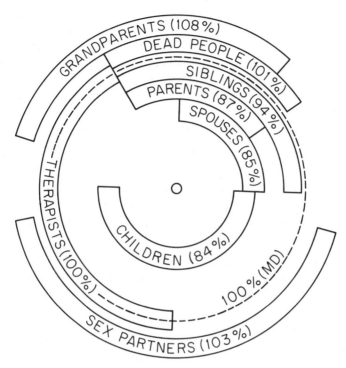

Figure 2-2. A composite model of areas of preferred placement. Distances and locations are approximate. The dotted line shows where the mean distance (100%) in such a model would lie; the figures in brackets indicate the relative distances for each category of "significant people."

Table 2-2
Areas of Preferred Placement (*N* = 982)

Categories of Significant People	Location (o'clock)	Distance (in % of "Standard distance")		*N*
		Mean	Range	
1. Parents	11–2 ¹²/₆	87	70–110	215
2. Grandparents	9:30–1:30 ³/5	108	87–125	66
3. Siblings	11–3 2³⁰/3³⁰	94	75–115	130
4. Spouses	12–3	85	60–105	88
5. Children	3–9 8³⁰	84	70–100	191
6. Sexual partners	3:30–8:30 ¹⁰ ⁶	103	70–135	111
7. Therapists	6–11 0 9 3	100[a]	70–125	45
8. Dead	11–2 7/1	101	80–125	136

[a] 111 for former therapists.

35

As can be seen, there are definite placement areas for the categories. Generally speaking, the past is placed above, toward the zenith. There we find the "dead people," or those in the distant past, like grandparents. Both groups are put far out. Closer in come the siblings and parents. The latter are concentrated on top, while the siblings spread out toward 3 o'clock, overlapping with the area of spouses, and approaching the area for children.

The bunching of parents between 11 and 2 o'clock has been so impressive that I called this area the *parent-sector* (sometimes also the dependency-sector). Within this sector, fathers are usually placed further away from the "self" than mothers.

Spouses and children are kept close to the "self," one group following the other around the clock. Sexual partners are placed further out and down; therapists are put to the left and at a neutral distance.

Several details are not apparent on the graph but are worth noting:

There is considerable overlap of the areas for the grandparents and for the dead. This is so because most grandparents have died. Dead parents (there are 57 in the sample) are not as far removed from the "self" as grandparents.

In the placement of children, there is a difference between boys and girls (which is significant on the level of 0.05). Boys are concentrated on the right side, girls in the lower half. This difference applies only to location, not to distance. There is, however, a difference in distance between natural and adopted or step-children. The latter are placed much farther out. Finally, there is also a difference in distance depending on the sex of the subject (the parent who drew the model). Mothers tend to place their children closer.

In the placement of spouses there is also a difference. Husbands usually put their wives farther from the "self" than wives put their husbands. Ex-spouses, that is, divorced or separated partners, are generally placed far out.

When one follows the progression of preferred placement areas around the model, two interesting observations can be made: First, the placement areas follow the progress of time, shifting, as it were, from the past to the present, and on to the future. Below the "self" they gradually turn into the past again and, in the zenith, they end with the dead.

Second, distance is used to indicate distance in time as well as in emotional attachment. The dead are moved out, and so are relationships which have grown old. Grandparents, former therapists, ex-spouses, and ex-sexual partners are all remote from the "self." In contrast, parents, spouses, and children—those with whom one lives and to whom one belongs—are held closer. They all find themselves inside the "mean distance" (as if this imaginary line provided a boundary for the present).

How distance in the model can be used to express emotional distance is best illustrated in the example of spouses. Their placement seemed to depend on the eventual fate of the marriage. Since our contact with the subjects continued after they took the test (in most instances for years), we were able to distinguish three groups: (1) If the marriage continued throughout the period of observation, the spouse was usually placed at a close distance. (2) If the marriage ended in separation, the spouse was placed farther out. (3) If the partners were already separated at the time of testing, the spouse was placed definitely far out.

Sequence of Objects

The sequence of objects is the succession in which they are drawn. It refers only to the objects and must not be confused with the order, that is, the succession of object, connecting line, and crossbar.

Important clues can be gained from the position an object holds in this sequence. However, there is not, and cannot be, a generally applicable pattern to the sequences in different models. In surveying our sample we therefore focused on the first positions only.

The first object placed into a personal sphere model was in 91% of the cases a "significant person." In 31% of the cases it was the mother, in 22% the father, and also in 22% a spouse. The tendency to select the mother as the first object was greater among women than among men (37% vs 23%). Conversely, the tendency to place the father first was greater among men (32% vs 13%). Evidently, not only is it a parent who comes to mind first, but sexual identification plays a part in this choice. For spouses, who were placed first, the difference between male and female subjects was negligible (18% vs 22%).

Other first objects were: children—selected exclusively by women; sexual partners—when the subject was single; and occasionally a sibling or a friend.

All first objects were overwhelmingly placed into the right upper quadrant (in 80% of the cases), and at a distance shorter than the mean distance (on the average, 85% *MD*).

These findings, which stem from the study for general tendencies (*N* = 136), were confirmed in the test–retest study. From the latter, we also know that first objects are exchanged, but only infrequently, and that the location of first objects—exchanged or not—remains impressively stable. Further details will be reported in Chapter 6.

In the next chapter, we turn to the variables which express the affective charge in relationships—the bonds and separations.

REFERENCES

Pecjak, V. Affective symbolisms of spatial forms in two cultures. *International Journal of Psychology,* 1972, *7,* 257–266.

Prelinger, E. Extension and structure of the self. *Journal of Psychology,* 1959, *47,* 13–23.

Sollod, R. The Personal Sphere Model: Norms, psychometric properties, and concurrent validity in a college population. Unpublished manuscript, Department of Psychology, New York University, 1977.

3
Test Variables:
Bonds and Separations

Bonds in relationships are represented by connecting lines, separations by crossbars which intersect these lines. We will first discuss the connecting lines.

CONNECTING LINES (*C*)

Connecting lines are drawn between the "self" and each object. According to the instructions, there should be from one to three such lines, depending on the strength of the attachment. In the vast majority of cases, the instructions were followed; in a few instances, the subjects "broke the rule." There is, for example, one model, from a schizophrenic patient, which contains no connecting lines; and there are two or three other in which individual objects were connected with four or five lines rather than three.

Much more frequent than these exceptions are variations in the way in which these lines connect. They can be "complete": reach from the border of the "self" to the border of the object; or "incomplete": fall short of these borders. It is hard to say just how precise one should be in these judgments. The personal sphere models are drawings, not drafted constructions. Minor inaccuracies will have to be expected, especially when the borders of the objects are not distinct, or the object is represented by only a label. Yet there are a convincing number of cases in which the connecting lines are so "incomplete" that the connection is simply not established. I have seen this in severe depressions and withdrawal reactions, and have tended to interpret it as a sign of isolation, and of feelings of loneliness and abandonment. It is likely that these lines are drawn short not by conscious decision, but rather under the influence of emotional factors which barely enter awareness.

The second variation is "penetration"—the connecting line enters the "self" or the object. A sample of this can be seen in *Example 1-2* in Chapter 1. In this model, the connecting lines between mother and "self" penetrate on either side. Like "incompleteness," penetration is a fairly frequent phenomenon. It is probably a sign of unresolved dependency, and an indication of insufficient separation at the boundaries.

An observation of Sollod's is pertinent in this context: He found a significant positive correlation between the number of crossbars in a model, and the presence of depressive affect (Sollod, 1977), and believes that it is the actual act of drawing these crossbars—the motoric emphasis of the act—which expresses the feelings.

There is reason to assume that the drawing of connecting lines and crossbars is largely under conscious control. Most subjects draw them with care or emphasis. They count them for individual objects, and sometimes alter them, making remarks like "This one does not deserve three connecting lines, only two." However, factors such as the total number of connecting lines or crossbars in the test, or incompleteness and penetration, seem to slip out of awareness and tap deeper feelings.

The number of connecting lines is important mainly for the evaluation of individual models. To compare the strength of attachments between several models, it needs to be brought into relation to the number of objects.

BOND INDEX (*C/O*)

The bond index is the ratio of the number of connecting lines to the number of objects. The range of this index is limited by the instructions. Theoretically it should go from 0.0 to 3.0. If someone draws no connecting lines to his objects, indicating, as it were, no bonds, the bond index becomes 0.0; if someone draws three connecting lines for every object, the bond index becomes 3.0 (we have one case of each in our sample). Table 3-1 shows the distribution of bond indices.

The median for the bond index lies at 2.0, and the interquartile range between 1.6 and 2.3 connecting lines per object. This means that, on the average, objects will be connected by two lines, with a variation of about half a line. Within this distribution, women tend to have slightly higher indices, and a slightly wider range. In other words, women show some-

Table 3-1
Bond Index (*C/O*)

	All Ss (N = 136)	Men (N = 56)	Women (N = 80)
Range	0.0–3.0	0.3–2.9	0.0–3.0
Q1	1.6	1.6	1.6
Median	2.0	1.9	2.0
Q3	2.3	2.3	2.4

what stronger bonding, and are more apt to choose extremes, that is, weak or intense attachments.

Adolescents also tend toward extremes. The highest bond indices in our sample, 2.9 and 3.0, were found in their models.

There is no correlation between the bond index and the object–ratio; that is, models with "people only" do not have higher bond-indices than models which contain mainly "ideas." Apparently, the size of the index is determined by the general tendency to feel strongly or weakly about attachments, rather than by the nature of the object. The only exception to this pattern was found in the tests of four psychotic women, who combined richness of "ideas" with a very low bond index.

The size of the bond index acquires particular meaning toward the ends of the curve. Bond indices below 1.5 need to be seen as a sign of increasingly poor attachments, and bond indices below 1.0—showing less than one connecting line per object—indicate a severe disturbance in the ability to form relationships. We have seen them only in the models of psychotic or borderline patients. In contrast, bond indices above 2.4 should be read as signs of intense, and in all likelihood very dependent, attachments. *Example 1-2* in Chapter 1 is of this kind.

CROSSBARS (*Cr*)

Much of what was said about connecting lines also applies to crossbars. According to the instructions, a subject may use up to three of these bars to indicate interruptions in relationships. Going beyond that number means a "breaking of the rule." However, while at least one connecting line has to be drawn to signify a bond, no such condition exists for crossbars. It is to be expected that no crossbars will be drawn for an object if the subject feels that there has been no "interruption" in the relationship. We have many examples of this in our material. It is another matter if there are no crossbars whatever in the *whole* model. Individual relationships may be free of interruptions, but it is unlikely that the same should hold true for all relationships in a sphere. Nonetheless, a sizeable number of models in our sample contained no crossbars (12.5%). We have understood this as a more or less conscious omission, which indicates particular difficulties in separations, and/or the direct expression of anger.

The opposite would seem to be true when more than three crossbars are assigned to an object. We have seen this, too, in a few models. In one instance, the number of crossbars assigned to individual objects reached 17, and the total number of crossbars 130 (see Chapter 7, *Example 7-7*). This was the test of a man who struggled with intense murderous and suicidal fantasies, and whose model contained several symbols of violence and voyeurism, such as guns, telescopes, and cameras. More than three crossbars, then, for individual objects, seem to mean that anger and aggression play a critical role in the relationship, and that the subject retains only tenuous control over these feelings.

When there are many crossbars in a test, it may happen that they outweigh the connecting lines. In such a case, the separation index will be greater than 1.0—and we can conclude that most or all relationships are endangered by rage. This does not necessarily have to be so, however, because the crossbars might be concentrated on a few objects.

Connecting lines and crossbars are brought into relation in the separation index, which reflects the balance of bonding and separating forces in a model.

SEPARATION INDEX (Cr/C)

The separation index is the counterpart to the bond index. It is computed by dividing the total number of crossbars by the total number of connecting lines. The index depends only on this ratio, and not on the number of objects. Its range, too, is determined by the instructions. If someone draws no crossbars, the separation index is 0.0; if he draws one crossbar for every connecting line, it is 1.0. Most separation indices are found within this range. Theoretically, though, the index could reach 3.0 when only one connecting line but three crossbars are drawn for each object.

I have to raise a point here, which applies to the crossbars and the separation index. The instruction to indicate interruptions in relationships by drawing crossbars is not as easily understood as the instruction to draw bonds. Questions about it are rather frequent, and usually are concerned with the ambiguity of the term. The word interruption has different meanings for different individuals. Also, most people will readily demonstrate positive attachments, but are reluctant to admit the more ambiva-

Table 3-2
Separation Index (Cr/C)

	All Ss (N = 136)	Men (N = 56)	Women (N = 80)
Range	0.0–3.0[a]	0.0–2.0	0.0–3.0
Q1	0.2	0.2	0.2
Median	0.4	0.3	0.4
Q3	0.6	0.5	0.7
± 1 S.D.	0.2–0.8	0.2–0.6	0.1–0.9

[a] 0.1–1.0 Without the Ss, who drew no crossbars, or more crossbars than connecting lines (N = 104).

lent and painful feelings connected with separations. From our experience, the crossbars signify distance—geographical and emotional, as well as distance in time; loss—of any degree, including death; grief, aggression, hostility, and ambivalence. All of these can be suffered passively, or wished for actively. They can be reduced to experiences of loss, ambivalence, and aggression in a relationship. None of these feelings goes without the other. "Interruptions" seem to be ambiguous because the feelings are ambiguous. Possibly for the same reasons, I have not been able to design a more clearly defined and readable measure which would still be simple to use. I believe that the separation index should be kept as it is, an expression of the overall balance between attaching and interfering forces in the personal sphere. In each case, one will have to determine from the larger picture which of the possible feelings is prevalent.*

The obtained range of the separation index (Table 3-2) is what it should be theoretically, namely, 0.0–3.0. However, this statement needs to be qualified. A full one-eighth (17) of the subjects had separation indexes of 0.0 because they drew no crossbars, and another eighth (15) had separation indexes above 1.0 because they indicated more interruptions than bonds. The remaining 75% (N = 104) are concentrated between 0.1 and 1.0, and show a fairly normal distribution. The medium for the whole sample (N = 136) is 0.4, and the interquartile values are 0.2 and 0.6. If one uses ± 1 S.D., the outside values become 0.2 and 0.8, respectively.

This means that, on the average, the separating forces have about half the strength of the bonding forces. From clinical experience, it seems that separation indices of 0.2 and 0.8 already represent extremes, and that in looking for "normality" one should draw the range narrower, from 0.3 to 0.6.

As in the case of the bond index, women present a slightly different

* Lyon experimented with several subcategories of separations (Cr). See Chapter 8, page 174.

curve. They are, on the one side, more likely to indicate no interruptions (12 of the 17 cases without crossbars are from women), and on the other side they are more apt to emphasize interruptions, as is evidenced by their higher values for the median and $Q3$.

Psychotic subjects frequently had very low or very high separation indices (0.0, 0.1, or 1.0 plus). In general, though, the index was not related to diagnostic categories, but seemed to depend upon the individual constellation.

In evaluating the bond and separation indices, one has to keep in mind that these measures cannot be taken as absolutes, and that differences of one-tenth of a decimal are not meaningful. What matters is the gross relationship of the averages.

To emphasize this point, we introduced a *ratio for the two indices (C/O:Cr/C)*. This ratio is expressed as 1:1, 2:1, etc. For example: If someone has a bond index of 2.2 and a separation index of 0.7, the ratio would read 3:1; or if the bond index is 1.6 and the separation index 0.2, it would be 8:1. Table 3-3 shows its distribution.

The figures in Table 3-3 show again that women are more inclined than men to emphasize either bonds or interruptions. This tendency is not strong, but clear enough to be evident. It is not related to diagnostic categories, but rather seems to be linked to conflicts over dependency. The findings for adolescents, which are similar to those for women, tend to support this explanation.

Table 3-3
Ratio of Bond Index:Separation Index (C/O:Cr/C)

	All Ss ($N = 136$)	Men ($N = 56$)	Women ($N = 80$)
Range	$1:3^a-15:1$	$1:2^a-11:1$	$1:3^a-15:1$
$Q1$	2:1	2:1	1.5:1
Median	2.5:1	3:1	2.5:1
$Q3$	5:1	5:1	5:1

[a] Reverse ratio because the separation index is greater than the bond index.

DISTRIBUTION PATTERNS

Distribution patterns are a device for ordering connecting lines and crossbars in a manner which offers an overview of their allocation to objects. In tests with few objects, one will hardly have to use these patterns—the distribution can be read directly from the model. But in tests with many objects, which often present a confusing array, distribution patterns prove helpful.

The following example* is taken from a test with 34 *O*, 50 *C*, and 27 *Cr*. The bond index is 1.47, the separation index 0.54. There are only "people" in this model, 11 of them relatives, the others friends and acquaintances. The model is very orderly, and looks like a construction. Yet it is impossible to get a feeling of the distribution because the objects are compacted, and their connecting lines crowd in on the "self."

C	0	1	2	3	more	Total
O	—	23	6	5	—	34

Cr	0	1	2	3	more	Total
O	25	—	3	3	3(4)	34

The distribution patterns reveal rather interesting conditions:

1. Attachments are generally weak; only 11 of 34 objects have more than one *C*.
2. Interruptions are focused on nine objects, on six of them heavily. In fact, three objects received 4 *Cr* each!

If we add to this that 14 connecting lines are "incomplete" because the picture is so crowded that they cannot reach the "self," it becomes clear that the subject has a very difficult time forming relationships, and that he has been "filling-in"; also that his anger is focused, and potentially explosive.

VALENCES

Valence is the ratio of bonding to separating forces for individual objects. It does for them what the separation index does for the whole model. However, while the separation index is expressed as a fraction of 1.0, valences reflect the actual balance, for example, 2*Cr*/3*C*. They show us, as it were, the affective loading of a relationship.

Valences can be useful in comparing different objects within a model, but they are really important, in fact indispensable, for following the changes in affective charge over time. We have three measures for evaluating the relationship to individual objects: location, distance, and the combination of crossbars and connecting lines, that is, the valence. Our retest study has shown that of these three, the valence is the most sensitive. Location changes very little between tests and retests, distance changes some, and valence changes fairly frequently. This is, I assume, as

---

* See Chapter 7, *Example 7-8.*

it should be. Connecting lines and crossbars were conceived in order to register affective loads. That distance and, in a different way, location, may also do that, has been a finding.

The changes that the valence registers consist of additions and subtractions of connecting lines or crossbars. If, for example, the original valence for an object was $3Cr/2C$, and became $1Cr/3C$ on the retest, this shift clearly indicates a move toward a less ambivalent, more positive attachment.

In addition to registering shifts in individual relationships, it makes sense to count the number of changes for the whole model, that is, how many crossbars or connecting lines have been added or subtracted altogether. This number will show the degree of change that has taken place.

The changes in valence, which one can expect from test to retest, differ from individual to individual, but on the average remain small. In the retest study, we found 117 additions and subtractions of C or Cr for 138 objects (in 29 models)—less than one change per object. It has to be added that not all objects contained in these models were included, but only the "significant people." Had we included all objects, the rate of change may have been different, but it is, of course, the affective change to "significant people" which counts.

As for the direction of change: Most frequent was the addition of connecting lines (42%), followed by the addition of crossbars (27%), subtraction of crossbars (19%), and subtraction of connecting lines (12%). In other words, changes tended to go in the direction of stronger bonds (61%, $+C$ and $-Cr$), rather than interruptions (39%, $-C$ and $+Cr$). This result was to be expected and hoped for, since most of the subjects in this study had been in treatment during the interval.

The following case will illustrate the changes in valence from test to retest.

The subject had 19 objects on his original test, seven of them "significant people": father, mother, wife, a sibling, two children, and a former sexual partner. The retest, taken after an interval of 15 months, contained 14 objects, six of them "significant": father, mother, wife, the two children, and the therapist. The sibling and the sexual partner had been dropped and the therapist added. For the five "significant" objects, which showed up on test and retest, the valences changed in the following manner:

		Father	Mother	Wife	Child	Child
Cr/C	Test	1/2	1/2	2/3	0/2	0/2
	Retest	2/2	0/2	1/3	0/3	0/3
		$+1Cr$	$-1Cr$	$-1Cr$	$+1C$	$+1C$

There are, altogether, five changes, one per object. Four go in the direction of stronger bonding, one toward greater separation. But the example demonstrates something else: Apparently valence will only be changed if the object is sufficiently significant and has to show up on the retest. If this inclusion is not necessary, affective change may result in removal.

One other finding from the retest study should be mentioned in this context.

Valence is only one factor, which expresses emotional involvement; distance is the other. Whether closeness or detachment are signified in the balance of valence, or in the distance of the object from the "self," seems to depend on individual preference. Valence is certainly the more frequent mode, and seems to be under greater conscious control.

REFERENCE

1. Sollod, R. The Personal Sphere Model: Norms, psychometric properties, and concurrent validity in a college population. Unpublished manuscript, Department of Psychology, New York University, 1977.

4

Test Variables: Distance and Gestalt

Describing the Gestalt of a design has met with difficulty. Originally, we attempted it by using bipolar adjectives, such as full–empty, close–far, orderly–disorderly, and open–closed. These impressionistic terms conveyed some feeling about a design but remained subjective. We have therefore combined them with objective measures which confirm and complement them. The first of these variables is the mean distance of objects from the "self."

MEAN DISTANCE (MD)

The mean distance is computed by measuring the distance from the center of the "self" to the nearest point of each object, and by dividing the sum of these distances by the number of objects. The radius of the "self" is 1 cm, so a distance of 5 cm means 5 cm from the center and 4 cm from the periphery of the "self." In practice, we use a sheet of transparent paper with concentric circles 1 cm apart, which is superimposed on the model. It proved impractical to measure distances of less than 0.5 cm. Also, we found that the nearest point of an object often corresponds to the length of the connecting lines, and in doubtful cases we have used this length to indicate the distance, provided, of course, that the connecting lines touch or come close to touching. When they are "incomplete" we measure the distance to the object itself.

Table 4-1 shows the distribution of the mean distances in our sample.

Table 4-1
Mean Distance (MD) (in cm)

	All Ss ($N = 136$)	Men ($N = 56$)	Women ($N = 80$)
Range	2.5–12.5	3.0–12.5	2.5–10.5
Q1	5.0	5.0	5.0
Median	6.0	6.5	6.0
Q3	7.5	8.0	7.5

The range of all distances, and thus of the mean distance, is limited by the size and form of the sheet. The highest mean (12.5 cm) indicates that all objects are placed as far from the "self" as the sheet will permit. In contrast, a mean of 2.5 cm tells us that the objects are drawn very close to the "self." The median of the mean distance lies at 6.0 cm, the Q1–Q3 range between 5.0 and 7.5 cm. The figures for the subgroups show that women tend to draw their models a little smaller.

The importance of the *mean distance* will become more apparent after we have described the next measure, the *mean difference in distance,* and the relationship between these two. I only want to remark that we can look at the mean distance as a sliding gauge which shows how the boundaries of a design move closer to, or farther from, the "self."

MEAN DIFFERENCE IN DISTANCE (MDD)

The mean difference in distance measures the degree to which distances in a model fluctuate, and conveys a picture of the boundary of the design. To compute it, we determine how far each object lies from the mean distance, and divide the sum of these smaller distances by the number of objects. Only positive values are assigned in this computation regardless of the position of the objects in relation to the mean distance. For example: A model has 10 objects. Their distances from the "self" are:

Object	Distance (in cm)	Difference from MD (in cm)
O1	6.0	0.2
O2	7.0	0.8
O3	6.5	0.3
O4	6.5	0.3
O5	5.5	0.7

*O*6	6.0	0.2
*O*7	7.0	0.8
*O*8	5.5	0.7
*O*9	6.0	0.2
*O*10	6.0	0.2

62.0/10	4.4/10
MD = 6.2 cm	MDD = 0.44 cm

In this case, the mean difference in distance is less than 0.5 cm, a very small value, since the mean distance is 6.2 cm. Small MDDs indicate that the objects in the model are equidistant from the "self," that the boundary is rigid, and that the Gestalt is likely to form a circle. Large MDDs mean that the fluctuation is great, that is, objects are placed close and far, the boundary is irregular, and the Gestalt is probably amoebic or starlike. Table 4-2 shows the distribution of the mean difference in distance.

The computations show that, on the average, the distances in a model fluctuate by 1.5 cm, and that the $Q1$–$Q3$ range is quite narrow—from 1.0 to 2.0 cm.

There are no significant deviations that depend on diagnosis, but again, there is a slight difference for women. They have a somewhat wider range; that is, they tend to show a little more fluctuation in the distances of their objects.

We also found a difference for young subjects. Only two adolescents moved outside the interquartile range—toward greater MDD. The rest remained well within these limits. Apparently, young people tend to keep their objects at fairly equal distances.

Table 4-2
Mean Difference in Distance (MDD) (in cm)

	All Ss ($N = 136$)	Men ($N = 56$)	Women ($N = 80$)
Range	0.25–4.25	0.25–4.0	0.25–4.25
$Q1$	1.0	1.0	1.0
Median	1.5	1.25	1.5
$Q3$	2.0	2.0	2.25

Since mean distance and mean difference in distance need to be examined together, we established a ratio similar to the one between the bond and separation indices. This ratio, MDD:MD, is expressed as a fraction. For a MDD of 1.0 cm and a MD of 6.0 cm, the ratio would read 1/6, and for a MDD of 2.0 cm and a MD of 4.0 cm it would read 1/2. In the first instance, the objects would fluctuate by one-sixth the length of the mean distance, and in the second instance by one-half. We found no ratio of 1/1, and only four over 1/12. Table 4-3 shows the distribution.

The usual fluctuation of objects around the "self" lies between 1/3 and 1/6 of the mean distance. Fluctuations of 1/2 or less than 1/8 the mean distance are rare. Actually, we found fluctuations of less than 1/10 only in male subjects. There were two models from men that showed no fluctuation whatever (MDD = 1/20). They could hardly have done better by carefully measuring the distance to each object.

Women have a tendency toward greater fluctuation. Their median is higher, and they rarely exhibit a pattern of rigid distancing. This finding corresponds to similar findings for the bond and separation indices. Neither young nor psychotic subjects showed any significant deviation from the general distribution.

The MDD/MD offers another way of visualizing the use of distance in the Gestalt of designs. A fraction of 1/9, for example, presents a rigid configuration, while a fraction of 1/3 indicates that objects are positioned at varied distance, and the boundary is flexible.

The mean distance (MD) has proved to be a very stable variable. It hardly changes, even after prolonged treatment. The mean difference in distance (MDD) is still stable, but less so. This would seem to mean that the size of a Gestalt, and possibly also its contour, are determined by deeply anchored factors; conceivably, they are of cognitive nature or are related to the body image.

As described above, the mean distance shows us how the boundaries of a design move closer to the "self" or farther away from it. The closer they come, the more we expect narrowness, restriction, need for protection, and, probably, depression; the farther they are pushed out, the more we suspect distance from objects, aggression, isolation, and suspiciousness–paranoia. I am much inclined to conceptualize these relationships in bodily terms, such as drawing oneself together, curling up, pulling a protective mantle tight, or pushing everybody away and keeping objects at arm's length, so that no one can touch or enter an intimate zone.

Little fluctuation in distance (1 cm or less) would indicate rigidity, while considerable fluctuation (2 cm and more) would be a sign of elasticity and adaptiveness, but possibly also turmoil. The corresponding values in the ratio MDD:MD would be less than 1/3 and more than 1/6. Of course, these signs must be evaluated in a wider context. A large mean distance, for instance, combined with little fluctuation and a sizeable number of objects, which are arranged like a wall around the "self," would speak for

Table 4-3
Ratio, Mean Difference in Distance: Mean Distance
(MDD:MD) (expressing the fluctuation in distances as a
fraction of the mean distance)

	All Ss ($N = 136$)	Men ($N = 56$)	Women ($N = 80$)
Range	1/2–1/20	1/2–1/20	1/2–1/10
$Q1$	1/3	1/3	1/3
Median	1/4	1/5	1/4
$Q3$	1/6	1/7	1/6

distance, rigidity, and guardedness. I have called this configuration the
"defensive wall."

How one is to reconcile these clinical impressions with the finding of
great stability in these variables, poses something of a problem. However,
two arguments may be helpful: The findings of stability stem from the
retest study, in which we used the *t*-test, to prove that the mean scores for
the whole sample were reliable. The rank-order correlations, which were
used to check for intra-individual change, did not show quite as much
sameness. In other words, there were intra-individual changes. Secondly,
we might assume that there are basic determinants for the Gestalt that are
typical for the individual, but that there is also an overlay which depends
on the present emotional constellation. Broadly speaking, depression
would tend to crowd a design and make it smaller; aggression would push
it away from the "self," increase its size, and possibly add features of
explosiveness and disintegration.

VOLLGESTALT

The concept *Vollgestalt* is used to gauge how much of the space on
the sheet has been utilized to develop a design. With it, we complement
the impressionistic description "full–empty," but do not replace it. The
variable is useful in assessing the completeness and roundedness of the
Gestalt, not in measuring its size, or in expressing the degree to which the
space has been filled.

To arrive at the degree of Vollgestalt we divide a circle into six
sectors, superimpose it on the model, and determine how many of the
sectors it occupies. Six sectors would be a "voll" Gestalt, one sector a
very partial Gestalt. Accordingly, we grade from 1 to 6 (6 = full).

We may find that a large Gestalt carries a low degree; that is, it is only
a partial Gestalt, while a small Gestalt may have a high degree—it is a

Table 4-4
Vollgestalt

No. of Sectors Occupied	Ss
1	0
2	4
3	13
4	26
5	41
6	51
	$N = 135$

Vollgestalt. A model which fills the space on the sheet, in extent as well as content, would need to have a Vollgestalt, a fairly high mean distance, a large number of objects or objects of large size, and show considerable fluctuation in the distances at which these objects are placed.

Table 4-4 shows the distribution of Vollgestalt. Practically no one had less than half the Vollgestalt. Roughly 30% of the models filled 3 and 4 sectors, another 30% 5 sectors, and 40% 6 sectors (i.e., had a true Vollgestalt). There has to be some correlation between the degree of Vollgestalt and the number of objects in a design. Models with fewer than 8 objects cover mostly 3 to 4 sectors, while models with up to 12 objects cover mostly 4 to 5 sectors. To cover 6 sectors seems to take at least 13 to 14 objects.

PRAEGNANZ

Praegnanz is also gauged rather than measured. It is graded from 0 to 6, 0 meaning no Praegnanz and 6 meaning the highest. To help us in determining Praegnanz, which, like Vollgestalt, is a concept borrowed from Gestalt psychology, we use three other variables:

1. The *degree of Vollgestalt.* The fuller the Gestalt, the higher the Praegnanz.
2. The *mean difference in distance.* The smaller this value, that is, the more the contour of the Gestalt approaches the form of a circle, the higher the Praegnanz.
3. The *form of the objects.* Circles, which repeat the form of the "self," speak for high Praegnanz. Labels, stick figures, faces and figures speak for low Praegnanz.

Table 4-5
Praegnanz

Degree	Ss
0	7
1	22
2	28
3	30
4	18
5	19
6	11
	$N = 135$

In combining these three measures, we attempt to give equal weight to each. For example: A Vollgestalt of 6, a MDD of 1 cm, and circles as objects would result in a high degree of Praegnanz, probably 5 or 6. In contrast, a Vollgestalt of 4, a MDD of 3 cm, and stick figures as objects would result in a low degree of Praegnanz, probably 2.

Table 4-5 shows the distribution for Praegnanz in our sample.

No Praegnanz and the highest degree (6) are rare. The median lies at 3, and it seems that in general one can expect to find lower rather than higher degrees of Praegnanz. Of course, this may have to do with the relative imprecision of the judgments.

I have come to believe that Praegnanz has much to do with conventionalism, and that its extremes should be considered pathological in terms of too much rigidity–conventionalism, or too little rootedness in established patterns. A high degree of Praegnanz points toward strong compulsivity and, in combination with other factors such as distance and general blandness of the design, speaks for a rigid, unquestioning approach with little capacity for insight. In turn, a low degree of Praegnanz speaks for flexibility or even looseness, and can be expected in lively, colorful, artistic, or already disturbed tests.

Vollgestalt and Praegnanz, like the mean distance and the mean difference in distance, are stable and show only minor intra-individual change. All these variables have to do with the Gestalt of the design. There is nothing in the instructions which would regulate them, or draw attention to their being part of the test. Therefore, it can be assumed that they are largely removed from conscious control. They tap deeper layers, it seems, which appear to be related to cognitive styles, concepts of personal space, and body image boundaries. I will return to this subject in the discussion of the retest study and in the chapter on theoretical considerations (Chapter 9).

5
Test Variables: Symbolisms, Order, Miscellanea; Summary of General Tendencies

The drawings and notations in personal sphere models could also be called *symbols*. I have occasionally used this term in order to indicate that objects have specific meanings. A house, for example, would stand for the patient's childhood home and represent an important memory, or a couch would be drawn to symbolize treatment and convey some idea about its place in the patient's life. In each such case, the meaning of the drawing was evidently conscious, and the use of the term *symbol* merely indicated that the object represented an underlying idea and not the thing per se. The situation is different with symbol*isms,* a term we have used to designate a separate variable.

SYMBOLISMS

While any drawing might be a symbol for a conscious idea, we have reserved the term *symbolism* for those drawings and notations which represent unconscious, or at least preconscious, meaning. *Example 2* in Chapter 1 contains four such symbolisms: O5, the patient's mother, who is drawn as a big blob; O6, and egg-shaped drawing which, without label, could not be recognized as a ship; O8, the husband, depicted as a mask; and O15, a pair of eyeglasses representing the therapist. In these drawings, conscious and unconscious elements are mixed. It can be assumed that the patient was aware of her intent to convey a sense of distance and aloofness when she drew her husband as a mask. It is less likely that she was also aware of projecting her own rageful and suspicious fantasies.

Similarly, the pair of eyeglasses for the therapist was certainly intended to picture an intellectual, impersonal attitude, but it also reveals the patient's lack of involvement and her inclination to relate to part rather than whole objects. Her mother and the ship are clearly symbolisms. Both speak for early, symbiotic relationships, insufficient separations, and unclear body boundaries.

There are other symbolisms in our tests that are not represented as drawings per se. Sometimes the connecting lines are arranged in a manner which permits us to arrive at conclusions about the patient's attitudes and fantasies. In one model, for instance, the connecting lines converge toward the objects and form points, as if they were piercing arrows. Another model (Chapter 7, Fig. 7-15) shows a similar arrangement in milder form. In still another model (Chapter 7, Fig. 7-8) the subject drew actual points for most of the connecting lines—some directed at the "self," others at the objects, many in both directions. When I asked this subject about the meaning of the points, he explained that they showed the direction of influence. This was no doubt his conscious intent, but inadvertently he had made the whole model look like a target full of arrows.

Other arrangements are more obscure. In one model (Chapter 7, Fig. 7-9) some connecting lines curve from the sides of the "self" toward the bottom of the sheet, terminating in objects which represent the patient's boss and friends. The shape formed by these connecting lines looks like an onion or a uterus. Contained within this shape are the patient's wife and children and, in part, the "self." Two other models (which will also be mentioned in a different context) show a circle drawn around the "self" at a radius of five or six centimeters. They are meant to represent these patients' mother.

It must have become apparent from these descriptions that symbolisms may be difficult to recognize and interpret. In our population they occurred rather infrequently. We found them in about 30 models, mostly from psychotic or adolescent subjects, occasionally in the model of an artist. More important than the *occurrence* of symbolisms is their *percentage* in relation to the total number of objects. Usually there were fewer than 10%, that is, only one or two symbolisms, in a model. We have seen higher percentages only in psychotics or borderline cases.

ORDER

Order is the name we have given to the succession in which the three basic test elements—the objects, connecting lines, and crossbars—are drawn. Labels were added as a fourth element, although in some tests they stand for the objects themselves.

This succession is stimulated by the instructions, which tell the subject: "Draw the objects, connect them, cross out the connections if there have been interruptions, and name the objects."

The *regular* order would be *O, C, Cr, L,* or *O, C, L* when there are no crossbars. Within this order a number of variations are possible. Labels may come before objects *(L, O, C, Cr)* or right after them *(O, L, C, Cr),* or objects and connecting lines may be switched *(C, O, L, Cr—C, Cr, O, L).* I do not believe that particular meaning can be attached to these switches. They occur in many models, except that the difference between no variations of order and many variations must say something about the way in which the subject approaches a task, that is, more or less systematically and rigidly.

More important are *irregularities* in order; I have differentiated two: (1) if a crossbar precedes a connecting line, which is very rare; and (2) delays—that is, if elements are added, subtracted, or changed after another object–complex was started.

Delays are very frequent. They are obviously triggered by associations and tell us something about the relationship between two objects (from the point of view of the subject).

When delays are very rare in a model, in which case the order would be very regular, this might speak for compartmentalization—a lack of associative connections. When delays are very frequent, this points in the direction of confusion and an inability to keep relationships apart.

Take *Example 1-3* from Chapter 1, for instance: The order for this model's 13 objects looks like this:

1. *O, L, C,* no *Cr*
2. *O, L, C,*   "
3. *O, L, C,*   "
4. *O, L, C,*   "
5. *O, L, C,*   "
6. *C, O, L,*   "
7. *C, O, L,*   "
8. *C, O, L,*   "
9. *C, O, L,*   "
10. *C, O, L,*   "
11. *C, O, L,*   "
12. *C, O, L,*   "
13. *C, O, L,*   "

It is obviously systematic. There is one switch of variables (5 to 6), a simple variation, which is continued. Crossbars are left out altogether.

On the other hand, take the following model: It has 11 *O,* 18 *C,* and 4 *Cr.* The objects are presented as neatly drawn circles and labels. But if we look at the order there is considerable lack of regularity:

1. *O*,   *C* and *L* delayed
2. *O*,   *C, L,* and *Cr* delayed
3. *O*,   *C* and *L* delayed
4. *O*,   *C* and *L* delayed
5. *O, C,*   *L* delayed
6. *O, C,*   *L* delayed
7. *O, C, L,*
8. *C, O, L,*   *Cr* delayed
9. *O, C, L, Cr,*
10. *C, Cr, L,*   *O* delayed
11. *C, Cr, L,*   *Cr* removed, *O* delayed

There are four switches in the sense of variation, which is not impressive. But there are no less than 15 delays. For 11 objects, this would seem to be much. Furthermore, everything was being delayed—connecting lines, crossbars, labels, even objects themselves.

This subject attempted to organize her model. She lined up the objects, as it were, before she decided how many attachments she had to distribute; and crossbars really gave her trouble. There are few to begin with, then two are delayed and one is removed.

It is important to check *what* has been dealyed or changed. Most frequently, crossbars are added or subtracted, fairly often also connecting lines. Less frequently, the objects themselves are altered. Certain aspects of faces or drawings may be emphasized, or labels added or corrected.

Secondly, one must note *when* an element is being changed, and in *what context.* These observations will contribute to the understanding of relationships and their interconnections.

MISCELLANEA

It remains to describe a few observations which cannot be fitted under any of the other headings.

a. It has been a general experience of mine that taking the test stimulates associations. Some subjects express them freely while working on the model, often with a considerable show of emotion. Others come back to them in subsequent hours, referring to one or the other aspect of the test and filling in historical detail. A few subjects explain each relationship as they move from one object to the next, tell stories, and describe events and people. I usually end up enlightened and feeling that I have been given a good, comprehensive, and edited case history.

b. In five instances, the subjects completed the personal sphere model on one side, then turned the sheet and continued on the reverse side.* Their "backside" models were looser, and showed a more intimate and fantastic content. It was as if these subjects, having finished the official task, could open up and permit a closer view of themselves. In evaluating their models, I have found it interesting to score the "frontside" and the "backside" separately as well as in combination.

   c.   Eight subjects made a face out of the "self" by drawing eyes and a nose in it. Three of them added bodies to this "head." I believe that this seemingly playful elaboration represents an attempt to confirm one's identity, or one's body image, or both. Two subjects did something similar, but more abstractly. They put their initials or first name into the "self."

   d.   Occasionally a subject will write not only labels but whole phrases or paragraphs. Evidently, this writing serves a need to explain more clearly and understandably what they are unable to convey by drawing. In this sense, it reflects the discomfort with an unfamiliar medium, and a defensive move into an accustomed habit.

   e.   I had the opportunity to test a case of fraternal twins, a brother and sister. Their personal sphere models showed some overlapping of objects, but otherwise little resemblance, except for one intriguing detail. When the brother had nearly finished his model, he drew a circle which encompassed all objects. He did not name this circle and could not explain why he had drawn it. When I tested his sister four years later, she drew the same circle and labeled it "mother." I feel certain that there was no communication between the twins about the test. The case has only anecdotal value and I cannot explain what happened, but I do know that the sister was more aware of the engulfing, almost symbiotic relationship their mother had with both of them.

SUMMARY OF GENERAL TENDENCIES FOR ALL VARIABLES

   In the following, the general tendencies of all the variables are presented in summary form.

Objects (O)

Number:

	All objects	*People only*
Range	6–43	1–40
Q-Median-Q3	10–*14*–20	8–*12*–18

* See Chapter 7, Figures 7-12 and 7-13.

Nature (P/I/Th):

50% of the models:	*"People only"*
50% of the models:	also *Ideas*, usually few, 1–2. More than 3 Ideas is many.

Tests up to 12 *O:* about 10% Ideas
Tests up to 20 *O:* about 25% Ideas
Tests up to 25 *O:* about 30% Ideas

Percentage of Ideas: over 30% indicates preoccupation. 50% and more only in psychoses.

Form:

Labels only	25%
Circles	40%
Stick figures	25%
Faces and figures	10%

Placement

Areas of Preferred Placement

Significant People	Location (o'clock)	Distance (in % of "standard" distance)	
		Median	Range
1. Parents	11–2*	87	70–110
2. Grandparents	9:30–1:30	108	87–125
3. Siblings	11–3	94	75–115
4. Spouses	12–3	85	60–105
5. Children	3–9	84	70–100
6. Sexual partners	3:30–8:30	103	70–135
7. Therapists	6–11	100	70–125
8. Dead	11–2	101	80–125

*Parent or dependency sector

Sequence—First Objects:
The first object is almost always a "significant person."

	All Ss	Men	Women
Mother	31%	23%	37%
Father	22%	32%	13%
Spouse	22%	18%	22%
Others	25%*		

* (siblings, children—by women, sexual partners—by single subjects, friends)

Bond Index (*C/O*)

	All Ss	Men	Women
Range	0.0–3.0	0.3–2.9	0.0–3.0
*Q*1–Median–*Q*3	1.6–*2.0*–2.3	1.6–*1.9*–2.3	1.6–*2.0*2.0–2.4

Separation Index (*Cr/C*)

	All Ss	Men	Women
Range	0.0–3.0	0.0–2.0	0.0–3.0
*Q*1–Median–*Q*3			
± 1 S.D.	0.2–0.8	0.2–0.6	0.1–0.9

Ratio of Bond-Index to Separation Index (*C/O:Cr/C*)

	All Ss	Men	Women
Range	1:3–15:1	1:2–11:1	1:3–15:1
*Q*1–Median–*Q*3	2:1–*2.5:1*–5:1	2:1–*3:1*–5:1	1.5:1–*2.5:1*–5:1

Distribution patterns: No norm
Valences: No norm, Minimum: 1 *C*
Maximum: 3 *C*, 3 *Cr*, Occasionally "the rule is broken" and more than 3 *C* or 3 *Cr* are being used for 1 *O*. Extremely rarely there will be no *C* for an *O*.

Mean Distance (MD) (in cm: use overlay)

	All Ss	Men	Women
Range	2.5–12.5	3.0–12.5	2.5–10.5
Q1–Median–Q3	5.0–*6.0*–7.5	5.0–*6.5* –8.0	5.0–*6.0*–7.5

Mean Difference in Distance (MDD) (in cm)

	All Ss	Men	Women
Range	0.25–4.25	0.25–4.0	0.25–4.25
Q1–Median–Q3			

Ratio Mean Difference in Distance: Mean Distance
(MDD:MD) (expressing fluctuation in distance as a
fraction of MD)

	All Ss	Men	Women
Range	1/2–120	1/2–120	12–1/10
Q1-Median–Q3	1/3–*1*/4–1/6	1/3–*1*/5–1/7	1/3–*1*/4–1/6

Vollgestalt (1–6 sectors)

	Range	2–6 sectors
	30% of the models	3–4 sectors
	30% of the models	5 sectors
	40% of the models	6 sectors

Praegnanz (0–6, gauged, use Vollgestalt, MDD, Form of *O*)

	Range	0–6
	Q1-Median-Q3	*2–3–4*

Percentage of Symbolisms: differs from model to model, usually less than 10% of number of O.

Order:

regular: *O, C, Cr, L; O, C, L;* or any variation
irregular: *Cr* precedes *C*
delays and *alterations*, after another object–complex has been started.

6
Reliability and Validity:
The Retest Study

In this chapter I shall report on the comparison study between tests and retests which was undertaken to examine the stability of the variables and their sensitivity for registering change. Differences between test and retest of the same subject should correspond to clinical change in the subject's own make-up, and in the nature of his relationships.

The stability of the test variables is directly related to the reliability of the test, and changes indicative of clinical change are essential for its validity and clinical usefulness.

Establishing the criteria of reliability and validity for a projective tool is difficult and will always leave room for criticism. We avoided overly narrow coding schemes that would have forced our data and deprived them of their richness and value as a source of clinical information (Krohn & Mayman, 1974). On the other hand, our approach provides statistical significance, and fulfills the requirements Rapaport established for projective techniques, namely: objective observation and registration, systematization and scoring of the material in a way which permits inter- and intra-individual comparison, and lack of knowledge on the part of the subject as to the significance of the test and test reactions (Rapaport, 1967).

The population of the retest study consisted of 29 subjects. Of these, 20 were female and 9 were male; 4 were juveniles, all others adults. The interval between test and retest ranged from two months to six years, with an average of 24 months. This interval did not necessarily correspond to the length of treatment, which in some instances was longer, in others shorter. Diagnostically, the population presented a mixed group, containing neuroses and psychoses as well as personality disorders.

The study was divided into two parts. In the first part, the mean scores of the variables for tests and retests were compared, using the t-test to assess their stability. Then Kendall's *tau,* a rank order coefficient, was used in order to see if and to what degree individual positions within the categories had changed. In the second part of the study, we investigated differences in the content of tests and retests, using qualitative as well as quantitative methods. For this purpose we selected two categories: the most important objects found in tests, that is, the "significant people"; and the "first objects" placed in a model. We looked for additions or subtractions, and for changes in placement or the affective value of relationships. We also checked if, and in which way, the "Gestalt" of the model might have been changed.

Some of the data to be reported have been touched on before. They will now be described in greater detail.

Tables 6-1 and 6-2 contain the ten test variables that lend themselves to statistical evaluation. We chose to use the bond index *(C/O)* and the separation index *(Cr/C),* rather than the number of connecting lines and the number of crossbars, because the latter would not permit meaningful comparisons; and we attempted, in the second part of the study, a statistical consideration of the placement of objects and their sequence.

The form of objects, distribution patterns, valences, and the order of test elements defy conventional statistical treatment, and are therefore not included in this investigation. The percentage of symbolisms is of only minor importance, and has also been left out.

Table 6-1 shows the mean scores, standard deviations, t-values and probabilities for the t-test, and Table 6-2 the *tau*-values and significances for the Kendall rank order coefficient.

In judging the stability of these variables, and thus their reliability, one needs to keep in mind the intervals between tests and retests, which were considerably longer than usually required for reliability measurements, and the active intervention of therapy during these intervals. If the variables prove to be stable, one should find this quite compelling.*

Two conclusions can be drawn from the data in Table 6-1. First, the mean values of the tests, and in most instances of the retests, are very close to the median values found to be normative for the total sample. Similarly, changes which did occur remained well within these ranges. This indicates that the test–retest group provided a representative subsample.

---

* Empirical evidence to be presented later will support this argument.

Table 6-1
Results of *t*-Test for Mean Scores in Test and Retest

Test (T) or Retest (RT)	Variable	Mean	Standard Deviation	t-Value	Probability (2 tail)
T	No. of Objects (14, 10–20)[a]	14.38	6.75		
RT		14.76	5.43	0.36	0.72
T	Bond index (C/O) (2.0,1.6–2.3)	1.96	0.60		
RT		2.05	0.57	1.05	0.30
T	Separation index (Cr/C) (0.4,0.2–0.6)	0.41	0.29		
RT		0.39	0.28	0.38	0.70
T	Ratio (C/O:Cr/C)[b] (5:1,3:1–8:1)	4.86	3.96		
RT		7.65	6.92	2.43	0.02
T	Mean distance (MD) (6 cm,4.5–8 cm)	5.77	1.91		
RT		5.94	1.99	0.47	0.64
T	Mean difference in distance (MDD) (1.5 cm,1–2 cm)	1.33	0.72		
RT		1.44	0.66	0.89	0.38
T	Ratio (MDD:MD)[c] (25%,17–30%)	23.59	12.41		
RT		24.76	10.16	0.57	0.57
T	Vollgestalt (5,4–6)	4.83	1.17		
RT		5.07	0.99	1.07	0.29
T	Praegnanz (3,2–4)	3.45	1.76		
RT		3.28	1.44	0.63	0.53
T	Percentage of ideas (10–25%)	9.89	22.75[d]		
RT		13.72	15.96	0.84	0.41

[a] In brackets: Normative values for median and interquartile range, based on 136 subjects.

[b] The ratio C/O:Cr/C is normally expressed as 3:1, 4:1 asf. Here only the first part of this ratio shows, e.g., *4.86*:1. The norms used in this computation did not include tests with negative ratios. They are therefore higher than those reported in Chapter 3.

[c] The ratio MDD:MD is usually expressed as a fraction. For statistical purposes, these fractions were translated into percentages.

[d] This very large S.D. came about through the unusually dispersed distribution.

Second, we find that there is very little change between tests and retests. The number of objects, the separation index, the mean distance, the mean difference in distance, the ratio between these two, and the Praegnanz changed so little that for practical purposes we can consider them unchanged. The bond index and the Vollgestalt showed some change, but it is slight and insignificant. The percentage of ideas changed substantially according to the means, but the change is not statistically significant and also not meaningful when one considers the usual range of "ideas." We expect to find about 10% "ideas" in tests with up to 12 objects, and 25% in tests with up to 20 objects. Here too, then, we find relative stability.

The only variable which has clearly and significantly changed is the ratio of bond index:separation-index. On the initial tests, this ratio was about 5:1—on the retests it became 7.5:1. This is the kind of change one would hope for because of the influence of intervening therapy, since it reflects a shift toward stronger bonding and weaker separating forces. Why this shift is not also reflected in the variables which constitute the ratio will be clarified later.

We now switch from the discussion of the stability of the mean scores to the examination of intra-individual changes. Table 6-2 summarizes the results of the rank order correlations. In contrast to the preceding tabulation, a significant correlation will now indicate that the positive coefficient could not be attributed to change.

All values in this table are clearly significant, except for the percentage of ideas and the ratio C/O:Cr/c, which are close to significant on the level of $\leq .05$.

Table 6-2
Results of Rank Order Correlation

Variable	Tau	Significance
Number of objects	0.45	0.001
Bond index (*C/O*)	0.31	0.011
Separation index (*Cr/C*)	0.28	0.017
Ratio *C/O:Cr/C*	0.22	0.061
Mean distance (MD)	0.37	0.003
Mean difference in distance (MDD)	0.38	0.003
Ratio MDD:MD	0.46	0.001
Vollgestalt	0.33	0.022
Praegnanz	0.49	0.001
Percentage of ideas	0.21	0.084

Three of the variables—the number of objects, the ratio MDD:MD, and the Praegnanz—show very little change in rank order and thus very little intra-individual change between test and retest. Mean distance and mean difference in distance show some change, but not much. As we come to the variable Vollgestalt, the rate of change increases. For the bond index and the separation index, intra-individual changes become fairly frequent, and in their combination, the ratio bond index:separation index, they become pronounced. Finally, the percentage of ideas changes more often than any other variable.

These results allow us to answer the question: Why were shifts toward stronger bonds and weaker interruptions significantly reflected only in the ratio bond index:separation index, and not in either of these indices alone? The bond index and separation index of individual subjects did register shifts, and actually changed fairly often, but their movements were not strong enough to find expression in the means of the whole sample. They reached significance only in combination.

Summarizing the findings from t-test and rank order correlation, we can say:

1. All variables, except the ratio of bonding and separating forces (C/O:Cr/C), are stable.

2. The number of objects is highly consistent from test to retest. Objects are rarely added or subtracted; or, more correctly, the range of objects is retained, even after prolonged intervals and under treatment.

    The same holds true for the variable Praegnanz—to a less certain degree, however—since this variable is not as precise.

3. The variables that show the greatest intra-individual change are the bond index, the separation index, and their combination, the ratio C/O:Cr/C. Other variables, which register considerable intra-individual change, are the percentage of ideas, which we found increased, and the Vollgestalt, which moved toward greater fullness.

4. The mean distance and the mean difference in distance indicate some change for individuals, generally in the direction of increased distance and greater fluctuation. However, the behavior of the means and the stability and rank order consistency of the ratio MDD:MD indicate that these changes are minor. In other words, the "Gestalt" of a design, which is measured by these two variables, tends to change little from test to retest.

5. The findings establish that the personal sphere model yields stable scores on this set of variables despite long intervals of time, is sensitive to changes, and registers them in a consistent and convincing

manner. Therefore, it appears that the test offers reliable and valid results.

In the second part of the study, we focused on "first objects" and "significant people." We wanted to know if, and to what degree, the composition of "significant people" would change from test to retest, and which "first objects" were likely to be retained. Also, we were interested in determining how the change in the emotional climate of relationships would be reflected in changes of placement and affective charge. The variables available for collecting these data were the location of objects (their place on the clockface), the distance from the "self" (expressed in percent of mean distance), and the valence of the relationship *(Cr/C).* *

First Objects

The "first objects" of the retest study were almost identical to the "first objects" of the larger sample from which we drew the normative data. Mothers were selected most often, followed by fathers, spouses, and children.

On the retests, 16 of the 29 subjects retained their "first object," and 13 exchanged it. The exchanges did not follow any pattern, but remained restricted to the narrow circle of immediate-family members. For instance, one parent would be substituted for the other, or a child would be replaced by a spouse. The exceptions were two cases in which the therapist was moved into the place of the "first object" (previously the father), and one case in which a predominant idea (schooling) was replaced by a personal relationship (to the mother). The shift in each exchange reflected the subject's present emotional preference, and made sense in terms of his progress in therapy.

How much meaning one should attach to these exchanges is difficult to say. In fact, one may, in general, have to be cautious in estimating the importance of a "first object." From clinical experience, I am inclined to set this value high. On the other hand, there is little leeway in the sequence of first, second, and third objects and the positions in this sequence have to be weighed against other indicators, such as distance and valence.

The location of "first objects" remained impressively stable. In three-fourth of the retests we found them in the same area into which they were placed in the original tests (75% for those with the same "first object,"

---

* The valence is identical with the separation index, except that it is expressed as a ratio rather than a number, and refers to single relationships (see Chapter 3).

70% for those with a different "first object"). This was a narrow sector on top of the sheet: 67% of the "first objects" were located at either 12 or 1 o'clock, another 13% at 11 o'clock. In other words, there exists a clear and unchanging tendency to put "first objects" into that sector of the dial which we called the "parent sector." This tendency prevails whether or not the objects are, in fact, parents.

Distance and valence changed from test to retest, but not much, and by no means always. They remained the same or nearly the same for 10 of the 16 cases with the same "first object," and for seven of the 13 cases with a different "first object."

In summary, then, there is a fair chance that the "first object" of the test will be retained on the retest. The location of "first objects," exchanged or retained, tends to remain stable. Distance and valence may show changes, reflecting the altered emotional climate, but in general these changes will be minor.

Significant People

"Significant people" are the parents, grandparents, siblings, spouses, children, and sexual partners of our subjects, as well as their therapists and the dead in their models. They are "significant" because the subjects have a special relationship with them, and they are therefore likely to show up in most models, and can be traced from test to retest.

We found that not all categories of "significant people" could be included in all aspects of the test–retest study. In some categories, their numbers were too small to provide valid data. There were, for example, only 11 grandparents on tests as well as retests, and sexual partners were dropped in such numbers that it made no sense to track the remainder. We therefore limited the list of "significant people" to four categories: parents, siblings, spouses, and children. Together they gave us an N of 138, that is, 138 objects that were found on tests as well as retests. The data on changes of location, distance, and valence are based on this sample. For the report on changes in the composition of "significant people," we could still use all categories (N for tests = 210; N for retests = 222). Data for the dead are described separately.

CHANGES IN COMPOSITION

Before I describe the changes in composition, I want to draw attention to the fact that the total number of "significant people" changed very little—from 210 to 222. In the light of the previously reported finding that the number of objects remains stable, this may not seem surprising. However, it did not have to follow, since "significant people" comprise only a portion of the objects in a model. It is, therefore, of interest to look at the other figures: The total number of objects on the tests was 417, and on the retests 428; the total number of "people" on the tests was 369, and on the retests 365. In other words, the size of these groups also remained stable.

On the other hand, there were intra-individual exchanges: We found that on the retests 65 "people" had been subtracted, and 61 added (−4); and that "significant people" comprised 33 of the subtractions and 45 of the additions (+12).

This means that consistently about two "significant people" had been replaced by two other "significant people."

Looking at the categories in detail, we found that parents were always represented on tests as well as retests, whether they were alive or dead. (There were only three exceptions to this pattern: One subject included only his mother on both tests—his parents had divorced early in his life; another subject, a schizophrenic, omitted both parents on both tests; and still another schizophrenic omitted her parents on the test but placed her mother into the retest.)

Siblings and grandparents were added or subtracted relatively often. Grandparents were likely to be dropped, especially when they had died. Siblings were more likely to be added.

Spouses, like parents, were always represented on both tests, even when the subject was separated or divorced. Children were also always represented. They had been omitted on the tests in only two cases, but were added on the retests.

Sexual partners, and these were usually *former* sexual partners, changed a great deal. We found 35 on the tests, but only 18 on the retests. Twenty had been dropped, and three had been added. Those who were retained were most often the partners of single or divorced subjects.

Therapists were included on the tests by only four subjects; on the retests however, by 16.

In summary, the composition of "significant people" did not change for parents and spouses, and hardly ever for children. Siblings, who were omitted on the tests, tended to show up on the retests. Grandparents and former sexual partners were likely to be dropped. Therapists, in contrast, were likely to be added. Their addition is logical. When the initial test was taken the relationship to the therapist was beginning, by the time of the retest it had developed. Thus, we can say that the composition of "significant people'' did not change much, and that the changes that did occur reflected a move in the direction of greater orientation toward the present.

CHANGES IN PLACEMENT AND AFFECTIVE CHARGE

In this part of the investigation, we asked if and how changes in the emotional climate of relationships would be reflected in changes of placement and affective charge. To do this meaningfully, we introduced an additional variable: whether the relationship to a given object had clinically improved, worsened, or remained unchanged. Such an assessment could be made, since by the time of the retest the subjects were well known to the author. It was made blindly, that is, without recourse to the test data. There might have been some recall, but this seems unlikely considering the number and similarity of the data, and the interval of several years between their collection and utilization.

The results for location, distance, and valence are summarized in Table 6-3. The data permit several observations:

First, the changes in relationships that were clinically observed are reflected in changes in the test variables. Second, the variables changed more often and more impressively when the relationships worsened or improved than when they remained the same. And third, of the three variables, valence is the most sensitive.

It would seem justified, therefore, to say that these variables have validity as indicators of affective change and, by implication, of the affective loading of relationships.

For relationships, which became clinically *worse* in the interval between test and retest, the valence was changed frequently and quite drastically, mostly through the addition of *Cr*. Distance was also changed quite often. It tended to be increased, that is, the object was moved away from the ''self.'' The location changed least.

For relationships, which remained clinically the *same,* changes were made less often, and if so, in a milder way. Location was changed in some cases, but major shifts were rare. Distance was increased as well as decreased, but usually only slightly. The valence was changed rather infrequently, most often through the addition of *C*.

Relationships, which *improved* clinically, showed again major changes. Shifts in location were about as frequent as for worsened relationships, but not as extreme. Changes in distance occurred in about two-thirds of the cases, more often than not in the direction of decrease; that is, the object was moved closer to the ''self.'' Valence was also changed frequently; usually through the addition of *C* or subtraction of *Cr,* indicating stronger bonding.

Table 6-3
Changes in Location, Distance and Valence (N = 138 objects)

Relationship to "Significant people," clinically

Changes in Location (in hourly shifts)[a]

Variables	Worse (N = 18)	Same (N = 50)	Better (N = 10)
None 0–1	6 [33%][b]	22 [44%]	25 [36%]
Slight 2	4	10	18
Definite 3–4	3	10	18
Extreme 5–6	5	8	9
No. of changes	12 (8)[c]	28 (18)	45 (27)

Changes in Distance (in % of MD)[a]

Variables	Worse In-crease	Worse De-crease	Worse Total	Same In-crease	Same De-crease	Same Total	Better In-crease	Better De-crease	Better Total
None 0–10%	—	—	3 [17%]	—	—	20 [40%]	—	—	20 [29%]
Slight 10–25%	2	2	4	6	9	15	10	15	25
Definite 25–50%	1	1	2	5	1	6	5	1	6
Extreme 50+%	6	3	9	5	4	9	7	12	19
Total	9	6	18	16	14	50	22	28	70
No. of changes			15 (11)			30 (15)			50 (25)

Changes in Valence (Cr/C)[e]			
Ss with same	3 [17%]	33 [66%]	20 [29%]
Ss with change	15	17	50
No. of + Cr	11	3	18
No. of − Cr	3	5	14
No. of + C	6	13	30
No. of − C	5	4	5
No. of changes	25 (25)	25 (25)	67 (67)
Total No. of changes: all three variables[f]	52 (44)	83 (58)	162 (119)
Changes per S	2.9 (2.4)	1.6 (1.1)	2.3 (1.7)

[a] Change in location is given in "hourly shifts." If, for example, an object was placed at 1 o'clock on the test and at 4 o'clock on the retest, this means a shift of 3. Shifts of one hour were judged to indicate the same location—taking into consideration some inaccuracy in drawing as well as in pin-pointing location. Shifts of two hours were judged to be *slight*, of 3–4 hours *definite*, and of 5–6 hours *extreme*.

[b] Figures in [ ]—percentage of subjects with no change.

[c] Figures in ( )—number of subjects with definite or extreme change.

[d] Changes in distance are presented as percentages of the mean distance: 0–10% means *no change*, 10–25% *slight* change, 25–50% *definite* change, and over 50% *extreme* change. In addition, the direction of change is indicated, i.e., whether the distance to the object *increased* or *decreased*.

[e] We note first how many subjects changed valence and how many did not, and then list the number of added or subtracted bonds and interruptions.

[f] The last two lines in the table show the total number of changes, and the average number of changes per subject.

I have described how changes in relationships are reflected in changed values for the variables. We observed, as it were, their activity as they registered shifts. In reality, of course, the subjects expressed their changed affect by putting different loads into the variables. If we take these different loadings and apply them to the static picture of a one-time test, we can conclude that "poor" relationships will be indicated by great distance and preponderance of interruptions, and "good" relationships by close distance and an emphasis on bonds. In a way, this is like closing a circle and reiterating what was said at the outset. However, rather than state it as a basic assumption, we can now offer it as a conclusion based on observation.

Location has a different meaning. It seems to be the most stable of the three variables examined, and its choice seems to be less under conscious control. The best I can do at this point is to refer to the areas of preferred placement (see Chapter 2), and to the probability that location is related to the significance of the object.

The data in Table 6-3 give rise to another thought. Affective charges are expressed through valence and distance, more apparently through the former. Yet it seems that they can be expressed through valence *or* distance, and that it depends on individual preference which of these two variables will be used as the main avenue for the expression of affect. Whether such preference is indicative of differences in cognitive style has to be left open.

I have more recently examined how these same variables change under the impact of treatment. The sample was divided into subjects who had relatively short treatment (nine months on the average), and subjects who had extensive treatment (2–3 years). It was expected that the latter group would show greater clinical change, and that this change would be reflected in the retest scores. The PSM variables correlated were the same as for Part I of the retest study, plus three categories of "significant people," that is, relatives, sexual partners, and therapists. The results confirmed the expectations. The "longer treatment group" showed more changes in the PSMs, especially for the percentage of ideas and the ratio of bond index:separation index. The composition of "significant people" changed little, even after long treatment.

These findings would seem to offer further proof of the reliability of the test.*

---

* For similar results, see Chapter 8, p. 173.

THE DEAD

We found 39 "dead people" in the tests, and 38 in the retests. However, this stability in numbers is misleading. The category of the "dead" was one of the most active in terms of change from test to retest.

First, the composition changed. The 39 "dead" on the initial tests had been designated by 20 subjects, but six of these subjects eliminated nine "dead" on the retests. On the other hand, five subjects added eight "dead." This left us with 30 "dead," which showed up on tests as well as retests and could be used for the assessment of change.

We then asked: Who was dropped or added, who retained, and who had been included in the first place? With few exceptions, the "dead" on the initial tests had been grandparents or parents, and occasionally a spouse or a former therapist. Dropped were grandparents only, and added were also grandparents only. Dead parents or spouses were never forgotten on the test, and always retained on the retest.

The changes for the variables location, distance, and valence, are summarized in Table 6-4. Since the sample was small, we did not subdivide it accordingly to clinically apparent change in the relationships.

As can be seen, the rate of change between test and retest is high for the "dead," in fact, it is nearly as high as for relationships that became worse. Most impressive is the shifting of bonds and separations (C and Cr). There is not one single case in the sample where the relationship between these two was left unchanged. Next frequent in line, distance was changed. More often than not it was increased, and usually in a definite or extreme manner. In contrast, the location remained quite stable, more stable, in fact, than for any other category.

We should take another look, though, at the shifting of connecting lines and crossbars. In the previously described categories, presented in Table 6-3, we find certain emphases in this shifting: For relationships which became worse, the emphasis lies on increased separation; for relationships which improved or remained the same, it moves toward better bonding. No such emphasis can be found for the "dead." The changed connecting lines and crossbars balance each other. This is a curious result, considering the activity of these variables. I can think of two possible explanations: (1) that there has been a great deal of changing of C and Cr on individual tests, but that in the overall picture we happened to arrive at an equalization; (2) that the nineteen subjects in whose tests we found the "dead" provided some equalization themselves, that is, they separated more from one dead person but came closer to another. Clinical experience and a check of the individual tests tends to support the first view.

Table 6-4
Changes in Location, Distance and Valence for the
"Dead" (N = 30 objects)

Changes in Location (in "hourly" shifts)			
None	0–1	16	[53%][a]
Slight	2	5	
Definite	3–4	6	
Extreme	5–6	3	
No. of changes		14	(9)[b]

Changes in Distance (in % of MD)		In-crease	De-crease		
None	0–10%	—	—	6	[20%]
Slight	10–25%	4	6	10	
Definite	25–50%	3	1	4	
Extreme	50+%	7	3	10	
		14	10	30	
No. of changes			24	(14)	

Changes in Valence (Cr/C)		
Ss with same	0	[0%]
Ss with change	30	
No. of + Cr	11	
No. of − Cr	10	
No. of + C	10	
No. of − C	9	
No. of changes	40	(40)

Total No. of changes: all three variables	78	(63)
Changes per S	2.6	(2.1)

[a] Figures in [ ]—percentage of subjects with no change.
[b] Figures in ( )—number of subjects with definite or extreme change.

Changes in Gestalt

It remains to report an observation which cannot be adequately expressed by referring to the variables. The Gestalt of a model is a configuration which makes a definite impression, but resists measurement or description. We have attempted to capture it through such indicators as mean distance, mean difference in distance, Vollgestalt, and Praegnanz, and even through the number and form of objects. The approach enabled us to compare the dimensions of different Gestalten and conveys a rough image of their size and contour, but it does not convey the whole impression. There is simply no better way to compare the Gestalten of different models than to see them.

I should add that by "Gestalt" of a model I mean essentially the *contour* which is formed by an outline drawn through its objects. Connecting lines and crossbars, as well as the form of objects, may add to this picture. Figures 6-1 through 6-6 demonstrate the impression of a Gestalt and show how it changes from test to retest, or rather how it does not change.

In looking over the 29 pairs of tests and retests, it becomes apparent that there seems to be something very basic about the Gestalt. In many instances, it does not change, even if the retest model is modified in other ways. We had this impression confirmed by independent judges who were asked to rate the degree of change in Gestalt. Their combined judgment was that the Gestalt was the same in over 50% of the tests, that it had been changed but retained its basic congruence in about 30%, and that definite change was apparent in only 10%, that is, in two or three models.

Conclusion of the Retest Study

The retest study offers reasonable proof for the reliability and sensitivity of the personal sphere model as an instrument, and for the validity and usefulness of its results. The test has its primary utility in the area of object relationships, but it can also confirm and supplement clinical impressions and histories, and indirectly contribute to diagnostic conclusions (Schmiedeck & Kohlmann, 1975). Some of its data permit inferences about cognitive styles and about the manner in which space is perceived and organized.

Certain of the findings and observations of the retest study need to be discussed further, in particular the relation between variables and conscious control. This will be done in Chapter 9, within the larger context of theoretical considerations.

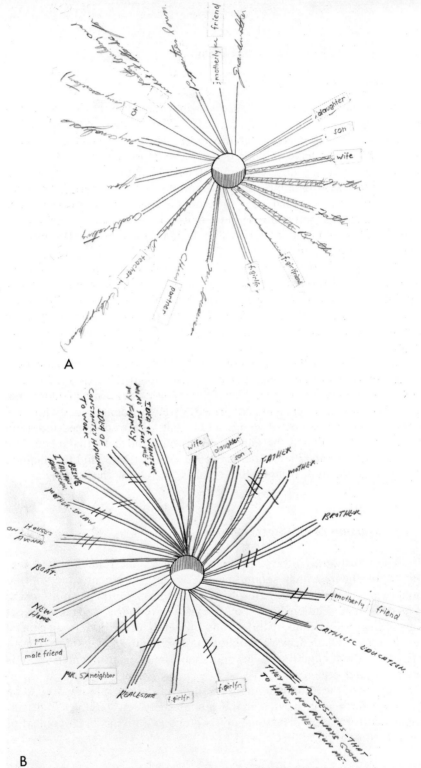

Figure 6-1. Gestalt unchanged. *A.* Test. *B.* Retest, 26 months later.

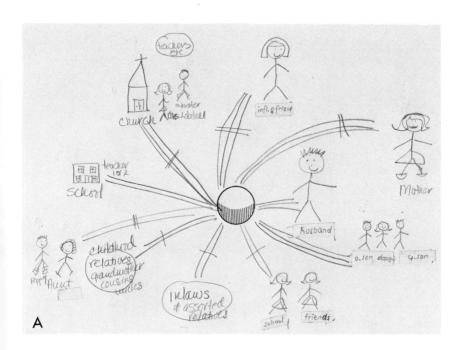

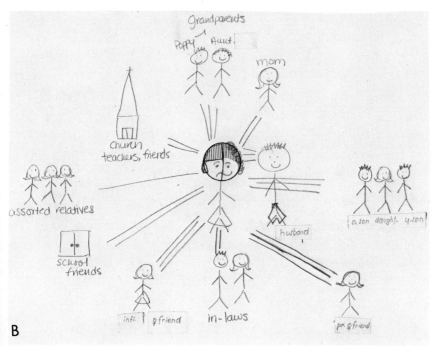

Figure 6-2. Gestalt unchanged. *A*. Test. *B*. Retest, 18 months later.

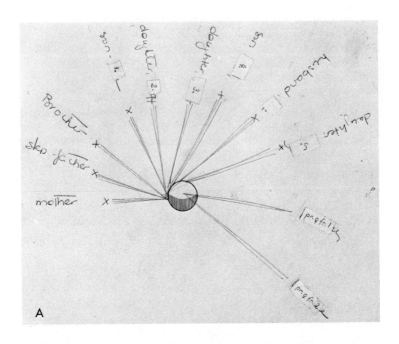

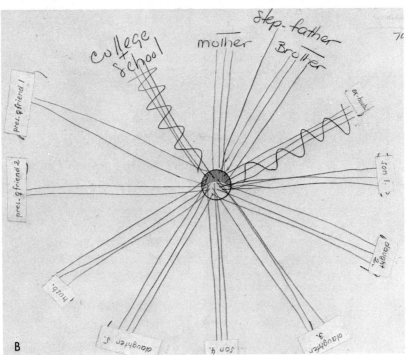

Figure 6-3. Gestalt shows some change, but retains basic character. *A*. Test. *B*. Retest, 32 months later.

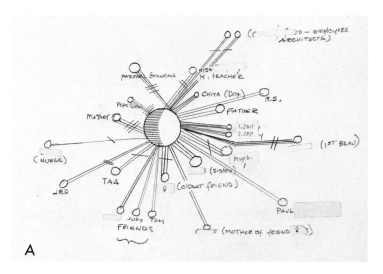

A

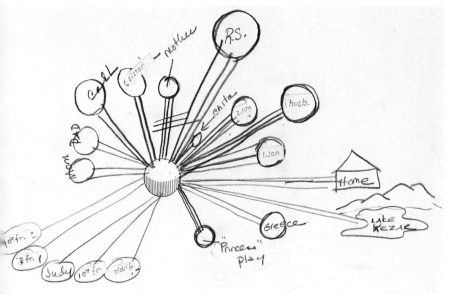

Figure 6-4. Gestalt shows some change, but retains basic character. *A.* Test. *B.* Retest, 26 months later.

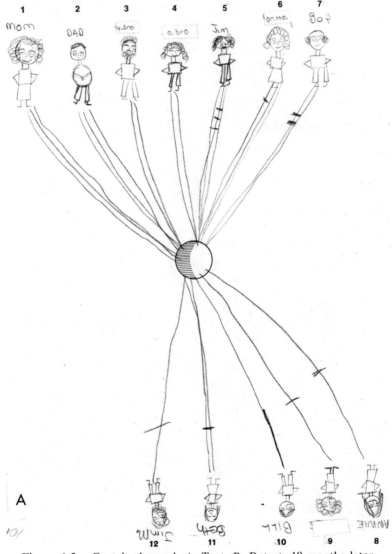

Figure 6-5.   Gestalt changed. *A*. Test. *B*. Retest, 19 months later.

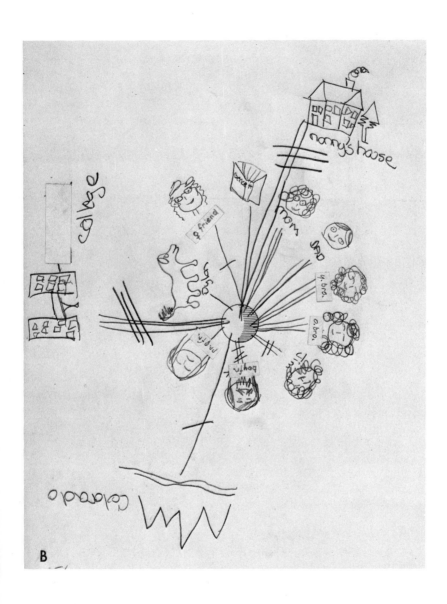

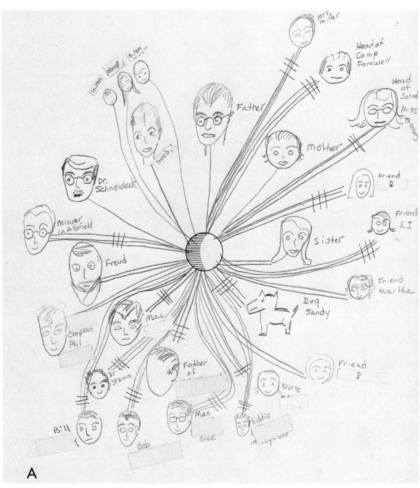

A

Figure 6-6.   Gestalt changed. *A*. Test. *B*. Retest, 20 months later.

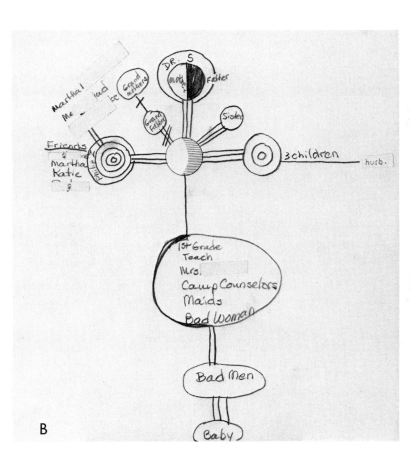

B

REFERENCES

1. Krohn, A. & Mayman, M. Object representations in dreams and projective tests. *Bulletin of the Menninger Clinic,* 1974, *38,* 445–466.
2. Rapaport, D. Principles underlying projective techniques. In M. M. Gill (ed.), *The Collected Papers of David Rapaport.* New York, Basic Books, 1967, pp. 91–97.
3. Schmiedeck, R. A. & Kohlmann, Th. Zur klinischen Validitaet des Personal Sphere Models. *Zeitschrift fuer Klinische Psychologie and Psychotherapie,* 1975, *23,* 151–162.

7
Examples

The examples in this chapter are ordered according to characteristic clinical features. These features correspond in large measure to the usual diagnostic classifications, but not always, and not in every detail. The appraisals of the personal sphere models are a conglomerate of conclusions about object relationships, comments of the patient, his behavior during the procedure, and about the manner in which he utilizes the building blocks of the test. The picture they convey may in some respects be narrower, and in others broader, than the assessment contained in diagnoses.

ADOLESCENTS

Example 7-1

This model is the production of a 22-year-old, single college student, a bright and sophisticated young man. He came from an intellectual family which was dominated by his mother, a depressed woman with a strong social facade and unrealistic ambitions for her children (the patient and his sister). The father was a compliant and dependent man, the atmosphere in the family one of polite cooperation and repression of feelings. Yet, for years the patient had been aware of strong hostilities underneath the pleasant surface. He had been pushed into a prestigious boarding school, where he remained isolated and unable to use his potential. After two years in college he dropped out. He was depressed, aimless, and contemptuous.

At the time of testing his essential relationships were to his girlfriend, to therapy, his sister, his mother, and his father—in that order. More important, possibly, he was attached to "things" and preoccupied with finding a direction in life.

Clinical diagnosis: Identity confusion and depression in an obsessional, intellectualizing, and lonely young man. (See Fig. 7-1 and Protocol 7-1.

SUMMARY OF OBSERVATIONS AND INTERVIEW

The patient worked quickly, with few hesitations. In the question and answer period, he expressed disdain over the crudeness of the design: "It's too simple. You just cannot express erudite things in this manner." I asked him why he had assigned only one connecting line to each object and added the others later. "There is one of each for value. I wanted to see the whole picture first." And then decide how you feel about each? "I can't remember how I did it. It's hard to say how I value these abstract lines." At this point he began to argue that he had drawn three connecting lines to his family in the first place (which he had not). The family was grouped together, he said, to emphasize that it was a unit, and the

Protocol 7-1

Order & Sequence (O,C,Cr,L)	Object[a]	Placement Distance[a]	Location
$O1,C1(1),L1$	Father, mother, sister	8,7,6	9
$O2,C2(1),L2$	Dog	8	8
$O3,C3(1),L3$	Girlfriend	8	10
$O4,C4(1),L4$	Car	8	11
$O5,C5(1),L5$	Treatment	7	1
$O6,C6(1),L6$	Work	5	2
$C3(2),C5(1),C1(2),Cr1(1)$			
$O7,C7(2),L7$	School	5	3
$O8,C8(1),L8$	Truth, beauty	4	6
$O9,C9(1),L9$	Doing the right thing	4	7
$C8(1),C9(1),Cr7(3)$			

Omissions: None

[a] Filled in after completion of test.

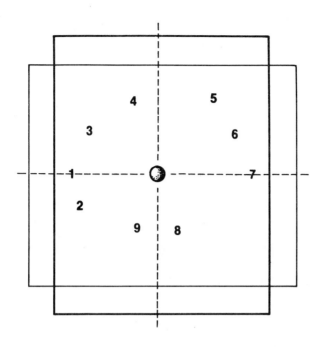

Valence[a] (Cr/C)	Comments	Remarks & Observations
1/3 for all	"Family here"	pauses
0/1	"These are things that are important to me now"	
0/3		
0/1		
0/2	"I should draw a picture anyway"	
0/1		
		now he adds C and Cr, delay
3/2		
0/2		
0/3		
		delay
		Again adds C and Cr
		Draws face inside "self"
	Time: 10 minutes	

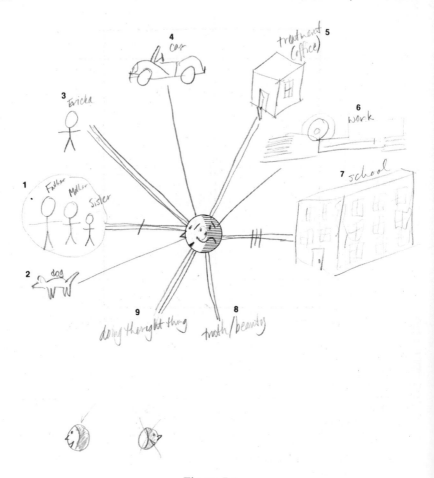

Figure 7-1

different size of the members indicated age and authority. I asked him whey he did not indicate sex differences. He answered angrily, "What was I supposed to do? Put a cock on my father and breasts on my mother? For the dog there is no official stick figure." Toward the end of the interview he commented that the test was interesting, but that it was work and that it intruded. Then, after a pause, he drew the two faces at the bottom of the page and said, "This ball in the middle is like a head. There is no body. These are two faces, also. The lighter side is the front side, the other makes no sense."

Scoring Sheet 7-1
Time: 10 minutes

A.	Impressions

1. *Gestalt*
2. *Feeling tone*
   (alive–dead; friendly–angry) alive; mixed but not unfriendly
   (see face in ''self'')
3. *Space and Distance*
   (full–empty; close–far) neither full nor empty; equal distance,
   not close or far
4. *Differentiation and*
   Sophistication
   (primitive–sophisticated) rather sophisticated
5. *Orderliness*
   (orderly–disorderly; fairly orderly, except the faces
   calm–wild) at 7 o'clock; fairly calm
6. *Openness* (open–closed) open
7. *Symbolisms* the two faces at 7 o'clock, face in ''self''

B.	Variables

1. *Objects*
   Number 9
   Nature *(P/I/Th)* 3/5/1, I% = 55
   Form stick figures and drawings
   Placement family clustered, very even distribution
   Sequence (Father, mother, sister), dog, girlfriend, car,
   treatment, work, school, abstract ideas

2. *Connecting lines (C)* 18
3. *Crossbars (Cr)* 4
4. *Bond Index (C/O)* 2.0
5. *Separation Index (Cr/C)* 0.22
6. *Ratio C/O:Cr/C* 10:1
7. *Valences* see protocol
8. *Distribution patterns*

C	0	1	2	3	more	Total
O	0	3	3	3	—	9

Cr	0	1	2	3	more	Total
O	7	1	—	1	—	9

9. *Mean Distance (MD)* 6.6 cm
10. *Mean Difference in*
    Distance (MDD) 1.0 cm
11. *Ratio MDD:MD* 1/7

12.	*Vollgestalt*	5
13.	*Praegnanz*	3
14.	*Percentage of Symbolisms*	about 20%
15.	*Order*	very regular, except *C* and *Cr* are delayed—with regularity

EVALUATION

This is not an obviously depressed picture. However, it contains very few personal relationships, and the "percentage of ideas" is high. His family is seen as a group, each single member receiving only one connecting line. The dog is a substitute for himself, the young child. The only strong relationship is to his girlfriend. It may express hope and dependency rather than fact. All this speaks for isolation.

There is a great deal of order in this model, of adherence to what is conventionally expected. This becomes evident more through the data than through the picture itself. The bond index is 2.0, the mean distance 6.6 cm, the Vollgestalt 5, and the Praegnanz 3, all values at or very close to the mean; and the order itself is very regular, except for the delays. On the other hand, the separation index is only 0.22, and the ratio $C/O:Cr/C$ is 10:1. This speaks for repression and the denial of aggression and strong feelings in general. The low fluctuation in distance (MDD:MD = 1/7) and the distribution of connecting lines in even groupings point in the same direction and emphasize his obsessiveness. There remain the face in the "self," the two faces added later, and the two "ideas" expressed in writing, which show his identity confusion and preoccupations.

Example 7-2

Little was known about this patient at the time of testing. He was 17, the youngest of five children, and in his senior year in high school. He seemed intelligent, yet his school record was abominable. The parents pressured him to improve his grades. He was noncommital, not verbal, rather passive, and hostile. Also, he was clearly attached to his mother, who seemed to be the more realistic and concerned parent, and doubtful about his father, whom he described as boisterous but not successful.

Clinical diagnosis: Adjustment reaction of adolescence.

The personal sphere model provided some interesting information (see Fig. 7-2 and Protocol 7-2).

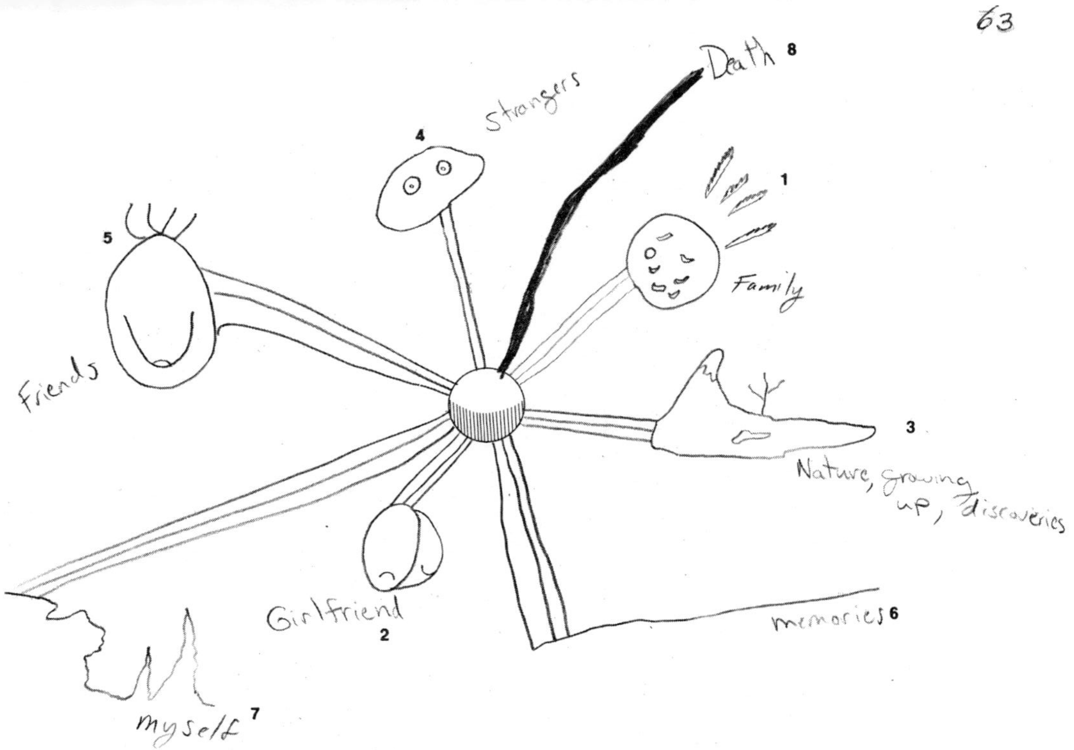

Figure 7-2

63

95

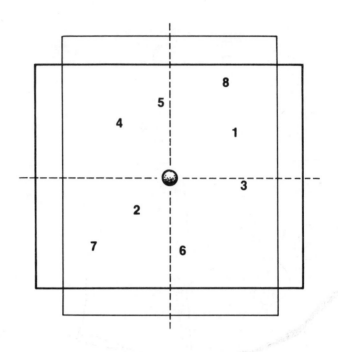

Protocol 7-2

Order & Sequence (O,C,Cr,L)	Object[a]	Placement	
		Distance[a]	Location
C1(3),O1,L1	Family	5	2
C2(3),O2,L2	Girlfriend	3	7
C3(3),O3,L3	Nature, growing up	4	3
C4(1)			
C5(3),O5,L5	Strangers	5	12
C4(1),O4,L4	Friends	7	10
C6(3),O6,L6	Memories	6	5
C7(3),O7,L7	Myself	12	8
C8(1),L8	Death	10	1

Omissions: None

[a] Filled in after completion of test.

SUMMARY OF OBSERVATIONS AND INTERVIEW

I am impressed with his drawing ability and the number of symbolisms. I ask about $O1$, the family: "This is kind of like the sun. A smile turned into loudmouth, which was my mother." Object 2 seems divided? "It's two-sided, a frown and a smile." The girlfriend also has two sides, just like the mother. Object 4, friends, has a smile, too. It is boyish, with its hair up. The patient has long hair, which his parents want him to cut. I ask him who these strangers are, with the big eyes ($O5$). He says that this is kind of an empty face—one does not know if he smiles. Later on, he adds that the stranger is himself.

The memories ($O6$) are about childhood, his girlfriend, perhaps some people who died. He remains noncommital, but I now learn that a few months ago, the mother of a friend died, and that some years earlier he was very upset when their dog was run over. Object 7 is himself; the line is "like a graph with ups and downs." And $O8$, death? "That started at my birth, a straight line leading up to now."

All of this is spelled out in an almost bland fashion. The only indication of stronger feeling comes when he reflects on $O1$. It stands for his family, I think mostly for his mother. He may have thought of it as a sun, he says, "because sunshine means happiness."

Valence[a] (Cr/C)	Comments	Remarks & Observations
0/3		large
0/3		subdivided?
0/3		
0/2		no Cr so far
0/3		works silently, delay
0/3		$C4,O4,L4$!
0/3		
0/1?		reinforces C

Time: 7 minutes

I also asked him why he did not draw crossbars. He thought he forgot them, and that the two smiles and the frown made up for them (this is in O4 and O2, his friends and girlfriend). When I suggested that he might want to add some crossbars now, he declined. No, he said, what was broken off mended itself. It was not gone forever.

Scoring Sheet 7-2
Time: 7 minutes

A.	Impressions	
1.	*Gestalt*	
2.	*Feeling tone* (alive–dead; friendly–angry)	mixed, alive and friendly, but also scary
3.	*Space and Distance* (full–empty; close–far)	not full; not close
4.	*Differentiation and Sophistication* (primitive–sophisticated)	almost artistic
5.	*Orderliness* (orderly–disorderly; calm–wild)	fairly orderly; not wild
6.	*Openness* (open–closed)	open
7.	*Symbolisms*	Very high, almost everything seems symbolic. This is a curious design, certainly not unfriendly or disorganized, but somehow disquieting.

B.	Variables	
1.	*Objects*	
	Number	8
	Nature *(P/I/Th)*	5?/3/0, I% = 37
	Form	drawings
	Placement	even distribution
	Sequence	Family, girlfriend, nature, friends, strangers, memories, myself, death
2.	*Connecting lines (C)*	20
3.	*Crossbars (Cr)*	0
4.	*Bond Index (C/O)*	2.5; excluding O7 (myself) = 2.86
5.	*Separation Index (Cr/C)*	0.0
6.	*Ratio C/O:Cr/C*	2.5:0
7.	*Valences*	see protocol

8. *Distribution patterns*

C	0	1	2	3	more	Total
O	—	1?	1	6	—	8

Cr	0	1	2	3	more	Total
O	8	—	—	—	—	8

9. *Mean Distance (MD)*   6.5 cm
10. *Mean Difference in Distance*
    (MDD)   2.0 cm
11. *Ratio MDD:MD*   1/3
12. *Vollgestalt*   6
13. *Praegnanz*   2
14. *Percentage of Symbolisms*   high
15. *Order*   regular, beginning with C. Delay
                                           around "strangers–friends."

EVALUATION

I learned quite a bit from this model and the follow-up interview. Most impressive is the picture itself. It has an artistic quality and tells more than he could say in words. Also—this became evident in the question and answer period—he became verbally more expressive after doing the test.

There is, first of all, the richness of symbolic presentations. They all deal with the dichotomy of closeness and loss, life and death. He is obviously depressed, fearful, and perhaps somewhat depersonalized. The main difficulty seems to lie with separations, which are experienced in extreme fashion. As serious as this threat may be, however, he is able to contain it. There is a great deal of fantastic elaboration, but the form of his design remains good, even pleasant, and there are no signs of real disorganization or disruption. The variables concerned with the design—MD, MDD, MDD:MD, and Vollgestalt, support this impression. Only the Praegnanz is a little off.

The model contains very few "people" even though the object-ratio reads 5/3/0. Of the five "people" in the test, one or possibly two represent the patient himself (O7 and O4), two more are groups and remain somewhat anonymous. Only the girlfriend (O2) is specified. Putting this together with three "ideas" for a total of eight objects points to isolation, conflicts in relationships, and preoccupation with narcissistically cathected ideas.

The bond index is high, excluding O7 (himself), very high. In contrast, separations are denied. This, and the emphasis on attachment (evident in the distribution pattern), show his dependency.

In summary, he does not want to leave home, does not know what to do with strangers, and feels isolated and cast out. He is depressed, possibly suicidal at times, but can fall back on good form and some sense of creativity and humor. Should the evidence of ambivalence and depersonalization increase, and the form suffer, there would be ground for concern.

COMMENT

The two tests presented show many of the features found in the personal sphere models of adolescents: The face in the "self" and the repetition of the "self" (directly in *Example 7-2* as a dog in *Example 7-1*), which are related to identity confusion and ego weakness; the high percentage of "ideas" and of "symbolisms," indicative of narcissistic preoccupation; the presence of "transitional objects" (the car in *Example 1*); the relatively high bond index and, more important, the low or nonexistent separation index, which point to dependency and, if combined with few or vague "people" objects, to isolation; finally, the more or less fantastic elaboration of themes, which is, I believe, normal unless it reaches a high degree (see *Example 7-13* on page 154, especially as it discusses the reverse side of the test.

DEPRESSION

Indications of depressive affect are, of course, present in many models. In the following two cases depression is predominant as a syndrome, and the tests show features that seem to be typical for this condition.

Example 7-3

The patient was a professional woman in her sixties. She was never married and had no children. Through an unfortunate combination of circumstances, she lost her job and was prematurely retired. She had a reactive depression of neurotic proportions which nearly paralyzed her. Her two main assets were close ties to some relatives and a stubborn insistence on remaining physically active.

Clinical diagnosis: Depressive reaction, moderate to severe, in a compulsive, well-organized, and intelligent woman (see Fig. 7-3 and Protocol 7-3).

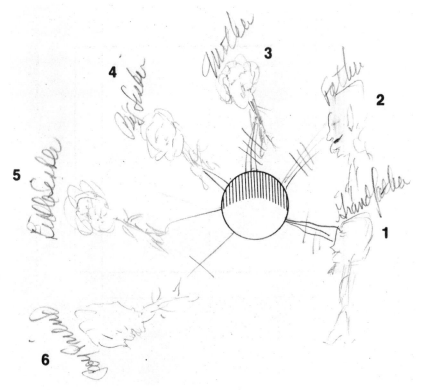

Figure 7-3

SUMMARY OF OBSERVATIONS AND INTERVIEW

The patient worked quickly. When she came to object 6 she began to think, but apparently there was no one she cared to add. After some more hesitation, the crossbars came. She assigned them to objects 1, 2, and 3, her grandfather, father, and mother, respectively. All three are dead. The relationship to her boyfriend, who also received one crossbar, goes back some 30 years. It was a good, satisfying relationship. Later on I learned that it was short-lived and that she did not know if this man was still alive.

Two immediate observations are of interest: I knew that her relationship with her older sister was strained, that in fact she had avoided her for years. Yet, this sister received two connecting lines. In contrast, the relationship to the younger sister was ostensibly good, and she was close

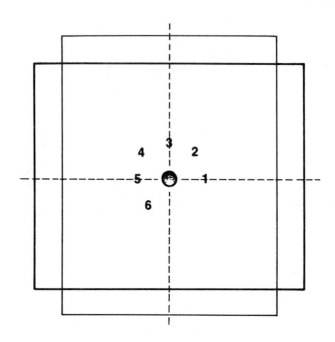

Protocol 7-3

Order & Sequence (O,C,Cr,L)	Object[a]	Placement Distance[a]	Location
O1,C1(3),L1	Grandfather	2.5	3
C2(1),O2,L2,C2(2)	Father	2.5	1
O3,C3(3),L3	Mother	1.5	12
O4,C4(1),L4,C4(1)	Big sister	1.5	10
C5(1),O5,L5	Little sister	2.5	9
C6(1)			
O6,L6	Former boyfriend	2.5	8
Cr2(3),Cr1(3),Cr3(3), Cr6(1)			

Omissions: Husband and children of younger sister, girlfriends, former boss.

[a] Filled in after completion of test.

to the sister's husband and children. However, she assigned only one connecting line to this relationship and omitted the sister's family. She also omitted a very important, long-term girlfriend, and a superior with whom she had worked for many years.

Scoring Sheet 7-3
Time: 7 minutes

A.	Impressions	
1.	*Gestalt*	shrunken, small
2.	*Feeling tone* (alive–dead; friendly–angry)	bland, sad
3.	*Space and Distance* (full–empty; close–far)	empty and close
4.	*Differentiation and Sophistication* (primitive–sophisticated)	not really sophisticated
5.	*Orderliness* (orderly–disorderly; calm–wild)	fairly orderly; trembling, shaky
6.	*Openness* (open–closed)	open
7.	*Symbolisms*	none

Valence[a] (*Cr/C*)	Comments	Remarks & Observations
3/3	"You want me to draw full figures? Name them as friend, relative, etc.?"	
3/3		some delay for *C*
3/3		
0/2		*C* delayed
0/1		erases *O5*, redraws turns sheet, thinks
1/1		waits, hesitates, now puts in *Cr*
	"I feel so impoverished to put so few people down. . . . For this minute this is it"	"You want more time?"
	"I think only of those who had real impact"	

Time: 7 minutes

Scoring Sheet 7-3 (continued)

B.	Variables

1. *Objects*
Number	6
Nature *(P/I/Th)*	6/0/0
Form	figures
Placement	close to "self," semicircle, evenly spaced
Sequence	Grandfather, father, mother, older sister, younger sister, former boyfriend

2. *Connecting lines (C)*   13
3. *Crossbars (Cr)*   10
4. *Bond Index (C/O)*   2.16
5. *Separation Index (Cr/C)*   0.77
6. *Ratio C/O:Cr/C*   3:1
7. *Valences*   see protocol
8. *Distribution patterns*

C	0	1	2	3	more	Total
O	0	2	1	3	—	6

Cr	0	1	2	3	more	Total
O	2	1	—	3	—	6

9. *Mean Distance (MD)*   2.2 cm
10. *Mean Difference in Distance (MDD)*   0.43 cm
11. *Ratio MDD:MD*   1/5
12. *Vollgestalt*   4
13. *Praegnanz*   2
14. *Percent of Symbolisms*   0
15. *Order*   all *Cr* delayed! Otherwise some switching but essentially regular

EVALUATION

The design is small, and shrunken. Everybody is held close and tight (the MD is very low), yet this mantle does not cover. The Vollgestalt is incomplete. Of the six people in the circle, three are dead and a fourth is practically dead. She is lonely and feels few attachments. She could have done better because in reality there are more people in her life. Apparently they are not available to her.

The separation index is high. This may mean that anger and aggression are close to the surface, but in this instance it seems to mean that the losses have been high. The bond index is good, and so is the ratio *C/O:Cr/C*. However, all the strong attachments are in the past, to the "dead." She seems to think a good deal about death, probably also her own. There are no "ideas," which is not a good sign for a woman of her intelligence and professional accomplishment.

The depression is evident. Her world has become small and shaky, and contains few securities.

Example 7-4

This test was done by a woman with a psychotic depression. She was in her late forties, divorced, and had two daughters. Her depressions began when she was around twenty, and reached serious proportions following the births of her children. She had spent many years in treatment with various psychiatrists, and at one point had been hospitalized.

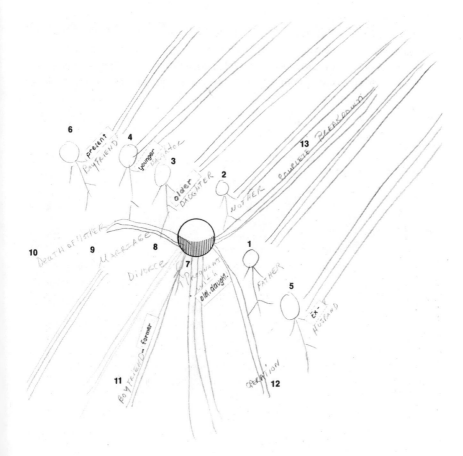

Figure 7-4

Some key events in the patient's life were known, and appear on the test: her mother's death some ten years earlier, her divorce, and an operation shortly before entering her present treatment. Cancer was suspected but not confirmed.

The patient lived a limited, depressed lifestyle, but was able to hold a job, and had a boyfriend. She had no hope, though, for remarriage. Two older sisters also suffered from depressions.

Clinical diagnosis: Manic-depressive illness, moderate, chronic, at this point about to enter an exacerbation, apparently in reaction to a recent operation (see Fig. 7-4 and Protocol 7-4).

SUMMARY OF OBSERVATIONS AND INTERVIEW

Most striking is the treatment of connecting lines. Many are not only "incomplete" but are also drawn away from the "self." All "people," except her former boyfriend, are thus disconnected. When I asked her about it, she said she did not realize what she had done and would at least want to connect her children. The relationship to the former boyfriend goes back many years. She knew him when she was nineteen. When I

Protocol 7-4

Order & Sequence (O,C,CR,L)	Object[a]	Placement Distance[a]	Location
$O1,L1,C1(3)$	Father	3	4
$O2,L2,C2(3)$	Mother	2	1
$O3,L3,C3(3)$	Older daughter	2.5	11
$O4,L4,C4(3)$	Younger daughter	4	11
$O5,L5,C5(3)$	Ex-husband	6	4
$O6,L6,C6(3)$	Boyfriend	6.5	10
$L7,C7(3),O7$	Pregnancy with older daughter	1.5	6
$L8,C8(3)$	Divorce	2^b	8
$L9,C9(2),C9(1)$	Marriage	3^b	9
$L10,C10(3)$	Death of mother	5^b	9
$C11(2),L11$	Former boyfriend	5^b	7
$C12(2),L12$	Operation	7	5
$C13(3),L13$	Breakdown	5^b	2

Omissions: sisters, all therapists

[a] Filled in after completion of test.
[b] Difficult to determine.

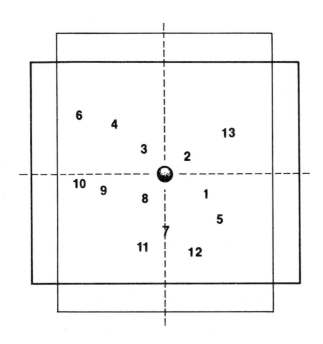

Valence[a] (Cr/C)	Comments	Remarks & Observations
0/3?	"If the relationships were detrimental they assume importance."	C away from "self"
0/3?	"I can't have 2 . . . 3 lines."	
0/3?		
0/3?		No Cr!
0/3?	"Too early for decisions."	
0/3?	"You want events too?"	
0/3		C connects now!?
0/3		
0/3?		3C after hesitation
0/3		
0/2		
0/2	"I don't have any more room."	
0/3		

Time: 16 minutes

asked where the "incomplete" connecting lines lead to, she answered,
"Into nowhere."

Two further observations: All "complete" connecting lines lead into
the dark area of the "self" and are related to "ideas" (except one). Those
from her mother's death penetrate into the "self." There are no
crossbars. The after-test interview was brief and offered little information.

Scoring Sheet 7-4
Time: 16 minutes

A.	Impressions	
1.	*Gestalt*	strange, uncommon
2.	*Feeling tone* (alive–dead;	dead
	friendly–unfriendly)	bland, maybe also angry
3.	*Space and Distance* (full–empty; close–far)	looks empty, even though it is not; confusing, close?
4.	*Differentiation and Sophistication* (primitive–sophisticated)	rather primitive
5.	*Orderliness* (orderly–disorderly;	rather disorderly
	calm–wild)	sad
6.	*Openness* (open–closed)	closed
7.	*Symbolisms*	?; C to people "incomplete," many point away from her

B.	Variables	
1.	*Objects*	
	Number	13
	Nature (*P/I/Th*)	7/6/0, I% = 46
	Form	stick figures, labels only
	Placement	"people" on one line, most C in space
	Sequence	Father, mother, daughters, ex-husband, boyfriend, pregnancy, divorce, marriage, mother's death, former boyfriend, opera- tion, breakdown
2.	*Connecting lines (C)*	37, but only 16 connect to "self"
3.	*Crossbars (Cr)*	0

4. *Bond Index (C/O)* 2.84, without "incomplete" $C = 1.2!$
5. *Separation Index (Cr/C)* 0.0
6. *Ratio (C/O:Cr/C)* 2.84 (1.2):0
7. *Valences* see protocol
8. *Distribution patterns*

C	0	1	2	3	more	Total (37)
O	—	—	2	11	—	13

Cr	0	1	2	3	more	Total (16)
O	—	—	2	4	—	6

9. *Mean Distance (MD)* 4.0 cm
10. *Mean Difference in Distance (MDD)* 1.6 cm
11. *Ratio MDD:MD* 1/2.5
12. *Vollgestalt* 6?
13. *Praegnanz* 3
14. *Percent of Symbolisms* ?
15. *Order* quite regular, some switching

EVALUATION

This is clearly a sad and rather disorganized picture. The sense of confusion derives mostly from the impression of disconnectedness, not from any particular lack of order. The patient had comprehended the instructions (I checked this with her).

The treatment of connecting lines is indicative of her almost total isolation, and her preoccupation with "ideas" ($I\% = 46$). These ideas concern the events she blames for her condition. It is interesting to note how her dilemma over dependency, preoccupation, and loneliness is reflected in the bond index (the separation index is 0.0, of course): If one counts all 13 O and 37 C, one arrives at a C/O of 2.84; if one counts only the 6 "connected" Os one arrives at the same value—2.83; but, if one includes all O and counts only the "complete" C, the bond index becomes 1.2. 2.84 is a very high, 1.2 a very low value.

A word needs to be said about omissions. Both sisters are missing, and none of the patient's therapists found entrance into her test.

COMMENTS

The features prominent in these two tests—a small, shrunken design, and numerous "incomplete" connecting lines—are fairly typical for depression. I am inclined to see the latter as a more serious sign.

Also fairly typical are the indices and their ratios. They express the conflict between dependence and isolation, and tend to be either high or low. However, high values for the bond index are often misleading. Strong ties lead not so much to "people" as to preoccupations (*Example 4*), or are counterbalanced by a preponderance of interruptions (*Example 3*).

Other variables, such as the MD, MDD, Vollgestalt, Praegnanz, and order, vary. Often they lie within the normal range. They can be used to gauge the extent of compulsive defenses which have been retained, of the anchorage in conventional form and reality, and of the degree of restriction. The impression of the tests is usually sad, dreary, and rather dead.

OBSESSIVENESS

Example 7-5

The patient was a teacher and student. He entered treatment in a crisis of indecision: Should he continue his already prolonged studies or enter his father's business? Behind this presenting dilemma, two others emerged quickly: He was married but had remained childless, and he suffered from a work inhibition which threatened to end his academic career.

The patient's father was a successful businessman, described as lively and aggressive, his mother a shy, withdrawn woman. He had one older and one younger sister, both married.

The patient was mildly depressed, but his indecisiveness and tendency to procrastinate were of greater importance.

Clinical diagnosis: Obsessive personality. (See Fig. 7-5 and Protocol 7-5.)

SUMMARY OF OBSERVATIONS AND INTERVIEW

By the time this patient had completed the test, I was exhausted and frustrated. I had repeatedly lost track of his placements and corrections, and knew that it would be cumbersome and time-consuming to reconstruct them. In addition, after working my way through the confusion, I could expect a disproportionately small amount of information. Anyone who has treated obsessives knows these feelings. That the same problems should arise in conjunction with using the personal sphere model is interesting.

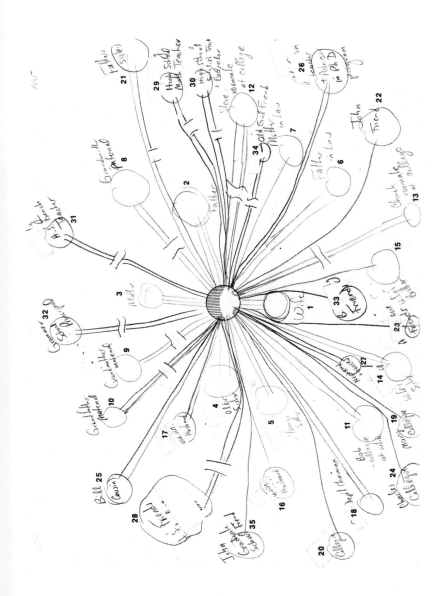

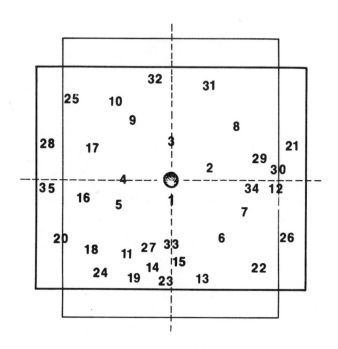

Protocol 7-5

Order & Sequence (O,C,Cr,L)	Object[a]	Placement Distance[a]	Location
O1,L1,C1(3)	Wife	2(4)	6
O2,C2(3),L2	Father	4	2
O3,L3,C3(3)	Mother	3	12
O4,C4(2),L4	Older sister	3	9
O5,L5,C5(1)	Younger sister	5	8
O6,L6,C6(2)	Father-in-law	8	5
C7(1),O7,L7 C5(1)	Mother-in-law	8	4
O8,L8,. . . ,L8,C8(2)	Paternal Grandmother	7	2
O9,C9(2),L9 Cr8(1),Cr9(1) . . . Cr8(1), Cr9(1)	Maternal Grandmother	6	11
O10,C10(2),L10,Cr10(2)	Maternal Grandfather	8	11
C11(2),O11,L11	Colleague (Competition)	9	7

The after-test interview was brief. The patient's first act was to draw eyes into the lower half of the "self" (they are hardly recognizable in the finished model). When I asked about them, he explained that he looked at the "self" from the top and the eyes indicated "what was in front of me." In other words, he looks directly at $O1$, his wife. Presumably, his plan of spatial organization was to have the present in front of himself, and the past in back. To a degree he succeeded, despite the confusion in placement. The patient started systematically, but as he went on, kept "filling in," and finally found himself crowded and struggling for space. This is a typical procedure, as is the equally unsuccessful attempt to place objects in chronological order.

Exceptional is the patient's innovation for separations. There are two types: In one type, two crossbars sever the connecting lines and leave empty space between them. He explained that this means a broken connection (e.g., to the dead grandparents, $O9$, $O10$, etc.), and that it indicates either a positive relationship, or that the object can no longer be seen (!). The other type severs one connecting line and lets the other

Valence[a] (Cr/C)	Comments	Remarks & Observations
0/3	"I should draw whatever I want?"	Draws unclearly in "self"
0/3		
0/3		
0/2		
0/2		
0/2	"The importance with the lines does not give enough range. One could also place closer or farther."	
0/1		erases 01 and moves it *closer*! Delay! C added to O5 erases, redraws
2/2		
2/2		
		erases and corrects Cr8 and Cr9.[b]
2/2		erases and corrects Cr10.
0/2		

Protocol 7-5 (continued)

Order & Sequence (O,C,Cr,L)	Object[a]	Placement	
		Distance[a]	Location
C12(3),Cr12(2),O12,L12	College roommate	9	3
C13(2),Cr13(2),O13,L13	College roommate	11	5
O14,C14(2),L14	Wife's sister	9	7
C15(1),Cr15?,O15,L15	Wife's brother	8	6
C16(1),O16,L16	Younger sister's husband	9	8
C17(2),Cr17?,O17,L17	Older sister's husband	6	10
C18(2),O18,L18	Department Chairman	13	8
C19(1),O19,L19	Colleague	12	7
C20(1),O20,L20	Colleague	14	8
C21(2),Cr21(2),O21,L21	Father's sister	13	2
C22(1),O22,L22	Friend	12	5
C23(1),O23,L23	Couple Friends	10	6
C24(1),O24,L24	Colleague	13	8
C25(2),O25,L25	Male cousin	11	10
C26(2),O26,L26	Advisor	13	4
O27,C27(2),L27	Nephews & Nieces	7	7
C28(2),O28,Cr28(2),L28	4 Highschool Friends	10	10
C29(2),Cr29(2),O29,L29	Highschool teacher	11	2
O30,C30(2),Cr30(2),L30	Highschool teacher	11	3
C31(2),Cr31(2),O31,L31	Highschool teacher	9	1
C32(2),Cr32(2),O32,L32	Grammar school principal	8	12
C33(1),O33,L33	2 friends	6	6
C34(3),Cr34(2),O34,L34	Former girlfriend	8	3
C35(1),L35,O35	Friend	12	9

[a] Filled in after completion of test.
[b] He invents his own sign for interruption. See interview.

continue (e.g., O29, a former teacher). It means that he rarely sees these people. They were important at one time but have no direct influence now. These devices are attempts to discriminate degrees of separation. They are unnecessary, and he inadvertently limited himself to the use of two crossbars per object. Had he been able to adhere to the instructions,

Valence[a] (Cr/C)	Comments	Remarks & Observations
2/3		erases *L*12, rewrites
2/2		
0/2		I am getting confused.
0/1	"There is a great variety of people wider out."	
0/1		
0/2		Draws *Cr*, erases, erases 1*C*, ends up with?
0/2		
0/1		
0/1		pauses, repairs *C*6 (father-in-law)!
2/2		
0/1		
0/1		now I really get lost.
0/1		
0/2		now he pauses and thinks.
0/2		
0/2		
2/2		
2/2		
2/2		erases and redraws *Cr*30, delay, does same with *Cr*29
2/2		
2/2		
0/1		
2/3		
0/1		
	Time: 32 minutes	

he could have used from one to three crossbars and would have had greater flexibility.

There are many "penetrations" in this model. They are indicative of his dependency, I believe, and of the vagueness with which he conceives ego and body boundaries.

Scoring Sheet 7-5
Time: 32 minutes

A.	Impressions	

1.	*Gestalt*	totally filled
2.	*Feeling tone* (alive–dead; friendly– angry	not lively; not friendly, if anything it's angry
3.	*Space and Distance* (full–empty; close–far)	crowded; mostly far
4.	*Differentiation and* *Sophistication* (primitive–sophisticated)	rather simple
5.	*Orderliness* (orderly–disorderly; calm– wild)	not orderly but confusing, crowded; not wild, but certainly not quiet
6.	*Openness* (open–closed)	closed
7.	*Symbolisms*	none

B.	Variables	

1.	*Objects*	
	Number	35 (!)
	Nature *(P/I/Th)*	35/0/0
	Form	circles and labels
	Placement	begins systematically, ends in confusion, "filling in"
	Sequence	Summarized: wife, family, followed by groups of friends, relatives, and coworkers
2.	*Connecting lines (C)*	65
3.	*Crossbars (Cr)*	24
4.	*Bond Index (C/O)*	1.86
5.	*Separation Index (Cr/C)*	0.37
6.	*Ratio C/O:Cr/C*	5:1
7.	*Valences*	see Protocol 7-5

8. *Distribution patterns*

C	0	1	2	3	more	Total
O	—	10	20	5	—	35

Cr	0	1	2	3	more	Total
O	23	—	12	—	—	35

9.	*Mean Distance (MD)*	8.8 cm
10.	*Mean Difference in Distance* *(MDD)*	2.5 cm
11.	*Ratio MDD:MD*	1/3.5
12.	*Vollgestalt*	6

116

13.	*Praegnanz*	4
14.	*Percent of Symbolisms*	0
15.	*Order*	frequent switches, delays and corrections of *C* and *Cr*

EVALUATION AND COMMENT

This test shows several typical obsessional features. There is, to begin with, the mass of objects, created by "filling in." Many of the relationships are not important (as can be seen in the distribution pattern), and the high number of ties does not lead to a strong bond index (1.86 in this case). The emerging picture is confusing and to some degree disordered.

Important are the frequent corrections, the erasing, redrawing, delays, and switches in order, which are indicative of the underlying ambivalence. Expressing the same conflict, but in a more controlled fashion, is a tendency to stick to the middle of the road, that is, the many objects with two connecting lines, or two crossbars, and objects in the form of circles and labels.

The design is not imaginative and not expressive. This, too, is typical. Unusual in this case is the lack of "ideas." Given the patient's intelligence and range of interests, one would have expected at least three or four.

ANXIETY

Example 7-6

The model I selected to demonstrate anxiety does so in an extreme fashion. It presents a picture of utter confusion and disarray, and its first impact is frightening. In my opinion, it conveys a message of impending breakdown. It is of particular interest that the degree of the patient's anxiety was not apparent clinically.

The patient was a single woman in her mid-forties, who had been twice married and twice divorced. At the time of the testing, she was about to separate from her lover.

Both the patient's parents had been immigrants. Her father died when she was 17, her mother three years before she came into treatment. The relations in the family were close and possessive. The patient lived

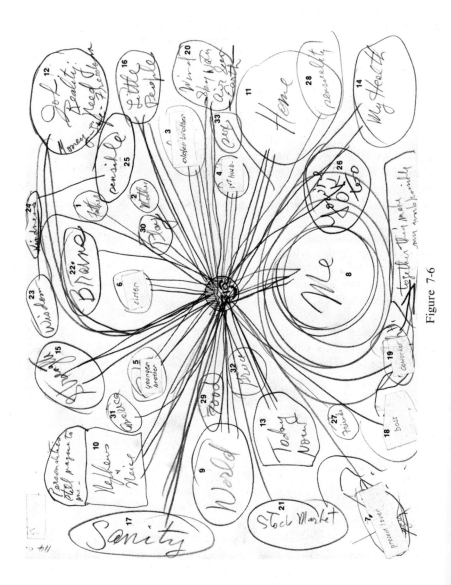

Figure 7-6

with her mother until nearly 30 years of age, and remained dependent on an older brother until she was well into treatment.

On the other hand, she was very bright and an excellent worker. By the time I met her, she was a respected executive in a field reserved for men, proud of her accomplishments and fiercely independent. Yet, she was doubtful and indecisive when it came to personal matters.

Clinical diagnosis: Anxiety reaction, moderate, with mild depression. After the test, this diagnosis was changed to: Anxiety reaction, severe. (See Fig. 7-6 and Protocol 7-6.)

SUMMARY OF OBSERVATIONS AND INTERVIEW

The patient started her model in a fairly clear and organized fashion. Soon, however, connecting lines began to cross each other, placements switched back and forth, and valences were corrected. By the time she drew *O*8 (me), huge and prominent, and emphasized by surrounding circles, I became concerned. She was obviously under much more pressure than I had thought. This sense of pressure, and eventually of confusion and impending disruption, increased as the patient proceeded. She must

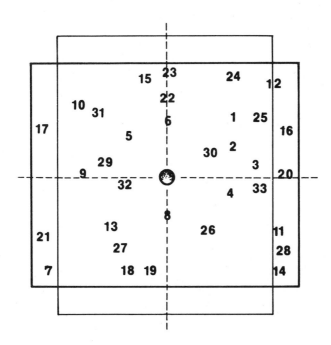

Protocol 7-6

Order & Sequence (O,C,Cr,L)	Object[a]	Placement Distance[a]	Location
$O1,C1(1),L1$	Father	8	1
$O2,C2(1),L2$	Mother	6	2
$O3,C3(1),L3$	Older brother	7	3
$L4,O4,C4(2)$	1st husband	5	3
$O5,L5,C5(1)$	Younger brother	5	11
$O6,L6,C6(1)$	Sister	4	12
$O7,L7,C7(1)$	Present lover	11	8
$O8,C8(5),L8$	Me	3	6
$O9,L9,C9(1)$	World	8	9
$O10,L10,C10(2)$	Nephew & niece	11	10
$O11,L11,C11(1)$	Home	8	4
$C3(2)C5(2),C6(2),C11(2)$			
$O12,L12,C12(3)$	Job, reality	12	1
$C9(2),C10(1),C4(1)$			
$L13,O13,C13(3)$	Today, now	7	8
$C14(2),O14,L14$	My health	12	5
$C15(3),O15,L15$	Strength	9	11
$C16(3),O16,L16$	Little people	10	2
$C17(3),O17,L17$	Sanity	12	10
$C18(1),O18,L18$	Boss	11	7
$C19(1),O19,L19$	Coworker	10	7
$C20(1),L20,O20,C20(2)$	Wind, sky	10	3
$C21(1),L21,O21$	Stock market	12	8
$O22,C22(1),L22$	Brains	8	12
$O23,L23,$	Wisdom	10	12 ⎫
$O24,L24,$	Kindness	11	1 ⎬
$L25,O25$	Sensible	9	2 ⎭
$C23–25(1)$			
$L26,C26(1?),O26$	You're OK, too (Therapist)	6	5
$O27,L27,C27(1)$	Friends	9	8
$L28,O28,C28(1)$	Sensuality	11	4
$L29,C29(1),O29$	Food	5	9
$L30,O30,C30(1)$	Play	4	1
$L31,C31(1),O31$	America	8	10

Valence[a] (Cr/C)	Comments	Remarks & Observations
0/1	"I'd leave it blank. Who's important?"	
0/1		crosses *Cs* with father
0/3		penetration
0/3		
0/3		
0/3		
0/1		
0/5		5 *C*!, big
0/3		No *Cr* yet!
0/3		*O* square
0/3	"This is too emotional."	huge
		Delay! Now she adds 2*C* to each of her siblings and *O*11
0/3		*C* to *O*12 bend
		Adds *C* to *O*9,*O*10,*O*4, crosses out *O*7, adds?
0/3		
0/2		
0/3		
0/3		
0/3		
0/1		
0/1		
0/3	"One romanticizes this guy"	
0/1		
0/1	"That enough"	I can't keep up.
0/1		1 *C* for all 3 *O*
0/1		the crossed *C* have become hopelessly entangled.
0/1		
0/1		
0/1		
0/1		
0/1		

121

Protocol 7-6 (continued)

Order & Sequence (O,C,Cr,L)	Object[a]	Placement Distance[a]	Location
L32,C32(1),O32	Country of parents' origin	4	9
L33,O33,C33?	Sex	8	3

Omissions: 2nd husband

[a] Filled in after completion of test.

have noticed my reaction, because at the end she looked up and said "I thought you knew."

I did—in the last phase of the test—lose track, and had to reconstruct the sequence of objects later on. In the question and answer period I was mostly concerned with sorting out. There emerged, despite the confusion, some order. The first seven objects represent her family, her first husband, and her lover. The second husband is omitted. The marriage to him was short-lived, an "erroneous attempt to find anchorage." Object 8 is a re-emphasis of the "self." She "broke the rule" and connected it with five lines! While it is a significant object, one should really not count it as separate from the "self," and calculate the bond index accordingly. Almost all of the following objects have direct reference to her and to the way she feels: She is concerned with her health and afraid of going insane (O14, O15, O17); she does not know what to do with the world (O9); and she needs to cling to reality, to today, to her work (O12). Her boss and a coworker (O18 and O19) make this possible. Some areas in her life are swirling and confusing: money, immature people, friends, sensuality, sex, play, food (Objects 21, 16, 27, 28, 33, 30, 29). It will take brains, wisdom, and kindness to sort them out (O22–25). Finally, there is the issue of feeling at bay. She needs a home (O11), and she needs to find her identity (O31, O32). I believe that she reemphasized this need by drawing a face into the "self" at the very end.

Valence[a] (Cr/C)	Remarks & Observations
0/1	
0/?	underlined? Next to 1st husband. Crosses 3C to home. Now she draws face into "self."

Time: 15 minutes

Scoring Sheet 7-6
Time: 15 minutes

A. Impressions	
1. *Gestalt*	it is frightening! Like an explosion.
2. *Feeling tone* (alive–dead; friendly–angry)	very anxious and angry, frightened
3. *Space and Distance* (full–empty; close–far)	too full; most *O* are far!
4. *Differentiation and Sophistication* (primitive–sophisticated)	primitive
5. *Orderliness* (orderly–disorderly; calm–wild)	totally disorderly, confused and disorganized
6. *Openness* (open–closed)	? one really can't tell, it's closed
7. *Symbolisms*	none

B. Variables	
1. *Objects*	
Number	32, "filling in"
Nature *(P/I/Th)*	12/20/0, *I%* = 62!
Form	circles and labels
Placement	begins with some order, eventually deteriorates into confusion

| Sequence | Family, lover, herself, and then a host of ideas, fears and preoccupations, in between some real relationships to friends and at work |

2. *Connecting lines (C)*   56
3. *Crossbars (Cr)*   0
4. *Bond Index (C/O)*   1.75
5. *Separation Index (Cr/C)*   0.0
6. *Ratio C/O:Cr/C*   1.75:0
7. *Valences*   see protocol
8. *Distribution patterns*

C	0	1	2	3	more	Total
O	1	15	1	13	1(5)	33

Cr	0	1	2	3	more	Total
O	33	—	—	—	—	33

9. *Mean Distance (MD)*   8.3 cm high!
10. *Mean Difference in Distance (MDD)*   2.25 cm
11. *Ratio MDD:MD*   1/4
12. *Vollgestalt*   6
13. *Praegnanz*   2
14. *Percent of Symbolisms*   none, except face in "self"
15. *Order*   frequent switches, delays, "rule break" for *C* (5C), crossing of *C*, penetrations!

EVALUATION AND COMMENT

The impression of erupting anxiety and increasing disorganization has been described. One needs to add that no object seems to be very close (the MD of 8.3 cm is high) and that, in general, relationships are felt in extreme ways. They are either weak or intense (distribution pattern). Most of the intense relationships are to her own thoughts, though, and not to people. The few personal relationships outside her family do not have much strength.

The model is "filled" with "ideas" ($P/I/Th$ = 12/20/0; the $I\%$ = 62). Nearly all these ideas mark fears and conflicts. She also lets us know what the main conflict is: there is not a single crossbar in the model. She seems to suffer intense separation anxiety, which forced her into a regression.

The bond index of 1.75 is rather low. If we extrapolate the twelve "people" in her model, and compute for them a separate bond index, we arrive at the same value (1.83).

In summary, we find that anxiety is expressed in disorder and confusion, in a tendency to show extreme values for relationships but a rather low bond index, and in a high percentage of ideas that deal with the patient's concerns and fears. Other factors, such as "penetrations," the face in the "self," and the repetitions of the "self," emphasize the threat to the ego.*

AGGRESSION

The following two models are described more briefly. They both are indicative, in different ways, of considerable aggression. I will concentrate on this aspect and deal with others only insofar as they have related bearings.

Example 7-7

This model has already been mentioned as an example of the extensive use of crossbars (Chapter 3, p. 42). It was done by a professional man of fifty, who was married and had three children. He was only

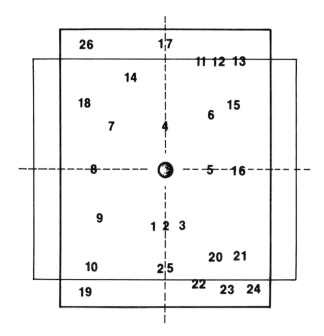

* This example shows one other feature which has not been mentioned so far. Lines and labels are drawn with much pencil pressure. I have routinely furnished a No. 2 pencil in order to make differences in pressure apparent. As one looks through the models one can intuitively sense these differences. It does not seem that they could be defined or quantified.

moderately successful in his work. His wife was an alcoholic, and he himself drank too much at times. He was a pleasant, shy, and depressed man, who had quiet interests and was well liked. Inside, he was a voyeur, hated women, and fought an intense struggle against murderous and suicidal impulses. (See Fig. 7-7 and Protocol 7-7.)

Protocol 7-7

Order & Sequence (O,C,Cr,L)	Object[a]	Placement	
		Distance[a]	Location
$O1,C1(3),L1$	1st son	4.5	6
$O2,C2(2),L2$	2nd son	4.5	6
$O3,C3(3),L3$	Daughter	4.5	6
$O4,C4(3),L4$	Wife	2	12
$O5,C5(3),. . .,L5$	Lover	4	3
$O6,C6(2)$	Gun	6.5	2
$O7,C7(1),L7$	Plants	5	10
$O8,C8(1),L8$	Boxes	6	9
$O9,C9(3),L9$	Office	6	8
$O10,C10(3),L10$	Therapist	9	7
$O11,C11(3),L11$	Mother	8	1
$O12,C12(3),L12$	Father	9	1
$O13,C13(2),L13$	Brother	10	1
$O14,C14(1),L14$	Sister	7	11
$O15,C15(3),L15$ $Cr15,Cr5,Cr11,Cr13$	Alcohol	8	2
$O16,C16(1),Cr16,L16$	Lover	6.5	3
$O17,L17,C17(2),Cr17$	Drawing	12	12
$O18,L18,C18(1)$	Photography	9	10
$O19,L19,C19(3)$	Telescopes	13	7
$O20,C20(3)$	Nude	8	4
$O21,C21(3),L21$	Nude magazines	11	4
$O22,C22(3),L22$	Sports cars	10	5
$O23,C23(3),L23$	Friends	13	5
$O24,C24(3),L24$	Early Work	14	5
$O25,C25(3),L25$ $Cr19,17,20-24$	Death	9.5	6
$O26,L26,C26(3),Cr26$	H.S. teacher	12	11

Omissions: former therapist, one sister and one brother

[a] Filled in after completion of test.

SUMMARY OF OBSERVATIONS AND INTERVIEW

The number of crossbars is overwhelming. They were drawn in two spurts. The first started after the label "Alcohol" ($O15$), in apparent reference to his own and his wife's drinking; the second followed the sequence of $O22$–$O25$, the skull. As he drew these objects, he com-

Valence[a] (Cr/C)	Comments	Remarks & Observations
0/3	"I should draw pictures?"	
0/2		
0/3		
0/3		
7/3!	"Funny, can't remember her name"	C "incomplete"
0/2		
0/1		
0/1		
0/3		
0/3		
13/3!		
0/3	"Damned near made a woman out of my father"	
17/2!		
0/1		
13/3!		
		hesitates, begins to cross out wildly. Delay!
7/1!		
8/2!		C "incomplete"
0/1		
14/3!		
14/3!		
3/3!		waits . . .
14/3!	"just occurs to me . . ."	
3/3!		
3/3!		
0/3	"It's all connected with death"	again, delayed Cr
14/3!		as an afterthought

Time: 35 minutes

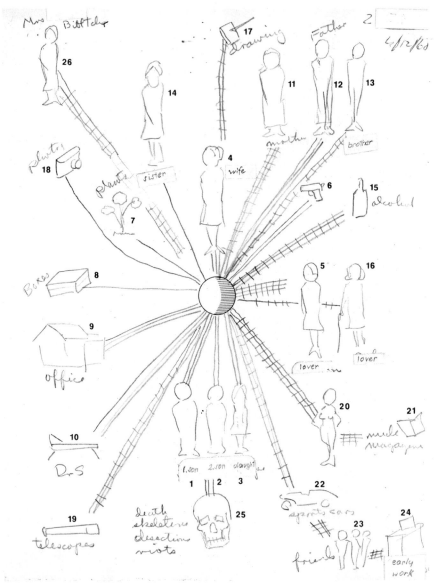

Figure 7-7

mented: "Just occurs to me . . . at one time cars have been extremely important . . . and behind the cars my friends . . . kind of the good old days . . . we all worked together. But . . . I always feel, in the background, death, in one way or another!" Then he crossed the friends, the car, the old days, and also everythinq which pointed to his voyeurism

(*O*19–21). Almost as an afterthought he added and crossed the high school teacher (*O*26).

When I asked about the many interruptions he said: "If you quit, you quit." And when I asked about the connecting lines which did not reach him, he pointed to death (*O*25) and said: "If it went right through here, it would destroy the figures (his children). . . . That would have been awfully messy." His final comment was "This looks like a hell of an empty page . . . not very much that's holding me . . . if this were an obituary it would be a pathetic one." (The patient died six months after he did this test—of a heart attack.)

Scoring Sheet 7-7

Time: 35 minutes

A.	Impressions	
1.	*Gestalt*	well planned and distributed at first sight
2.	*Feeling tone* (alive–dead; friendly–angry)	seems alive because of the drawing; angry, the cross-bars make for that
3.	*Space and Distance* (full–empty; close–far)	full; fairly close and very far
4.	*Differentiation and Sophistication* (primitive–sophisticated)	fairly sophisticated
5.	*Orderliness* (orderly–disorderly; calm–wild)	?, it is orderly, neat, but the crossbars make it restless
6.	*Openness* (open–closed)	rather closed
7.	*Symbolisms*	several: death head, camera and telescope for voyeurism, gun

B.	Variables	
1.	*Objects*	
	Number	26
	Nature *(P/I/Th)*	13/13/0, *I%* = 50
	Form	drawings, neat, good
	Placement	well arranged, on the whole distant, some groupings

Sequence	Immediate family, interests, therapist, parents, siblings, then he goes deeper into his feelings
2. *Connecting lines (C)*	63, several "incomplete"
3. *Crossbars (Cr)*	130!
4. *Bond Index (C/O)*	2.4, quite high
5. *Separation Index (Cr/C)*	2.06!
6. *Ratio C/O:Cr/C*	1:1!
7. *Valences*	many with multiple *Cr*
8. *Distribution patterns*	

7 objects with "incomplete" *C* !

C	0	1	2	3	more	Total
O	—	5	5	16	—	26

Cr	0	1	2	3	more	Total
O	13	—	—	3	10[a]	26

9. *Mean Distance (MD)*	8.1 cm
10. *Mean Difference in Distance (MDD)*	2.65 cm
11. *Ratio MDD:MD*	1/3
12. *Vollgestalt*	6
13. *Praegnanz*	3
14. *Percent of Symbolisms*	about 15%
15. *Order*	regular except delays and bursts of *Cr*

[a] These 10 *O* carry 121 *Cr*! Most of them have 13 or 14.

Example 7-8

Example 7-8 is the construction of a young, gifted engineer. He came from European peasant background, which was marked by primitive religiosity mixed with superstitions, by traditional feuds in the community, and by enforced closeness of the family. The patient broke away from home when he was in college, but was unable to shake this early influence.

He came into treatment because he could not be close to women, and also—although he would not quite admit to it—because he was paranoid. (See Fig. 7-8 and Protocol 7-8.)

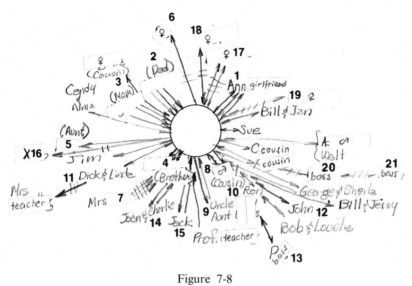

Figure 7-8

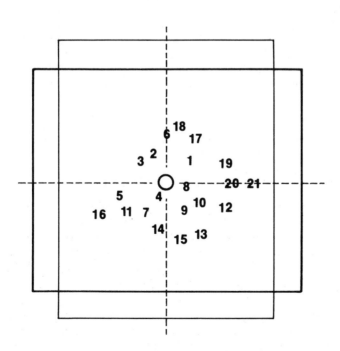

Protocol 7-8

Order & Sequence (O,C,Cr,L)	Object[a]	Placement	
		Distance[a]	Location
$L1,C1(3)$	Present girlfriend	2	1
$C2(3),L2$	Father	2	11
$C3(3),L3$	Mother	2.5	10
$C4(3),L4$	Brother	1.5	7
$C5(1),L5$	Aunt	4	9
$C6(1),L6,$ . . .,$Cr6(2)$	Girl	3.5	12
$L7,C7(3)$ . . .,$Cr7(4)$	Housekeeper	3.5	7
$C8(2),L8$	Cousin	1.5	5
$C9(2),L9$	Uncle & Aunt	2.5	6
$C10(1),L10$	Cousin	2	5
$C11(1),L11$	Pres. roommate	3.5	9
$C12(1),L12$	Coll. roommate	4.5	5

From this point on I was no longer able to follow him. The design was becoming too small and tight. Later on I reconstructed as much as I could. He drew altogether 34 objects. Those which are important for the understanding of his problems are listed.

$C13(1),L13$	Present boss	5	5
$C14(2),L14$	His children	3	7
$C15(2),L15$	Supervisor	3	6
$C16(1),L16,Cr16(2)$	Ex-coworker	5.5	9
$C17(2),L17,Cr17(3)$ ⎤	Girls who	2.5	12
$C18(1),L18,Cr18(2)$ ⎬	rejected	3	12
$C19(1),L19,Cr19(4)$ ⎦	him	3.5	2
$C20(1),L20,Cr20(4)$ ⎤	Former	4.5	4
$C21(1),L21,Cr21(3)$ ⎦	bosses	7	4

[a] Filled in after completion of test.

SUMMARY OF OBSERVATIONS AND INTERVIEW

This is one of the few models that were impossible to follow. The patient worked in such minute detail that I could not see what he did. He also worked very regularly, except for the delayed crossbars. Since everything was placed close to the "self" he soon began to feel crowded. When I asked him afterwards why he did not use the whole sheet, he reacted as if he had been oblivious to the available space.

There are only "people" in this model, but many of them are of dubious importance. The first object is a girl with whom he had a distant and troubled relationship; the following nine objects are members of his family. Most of the remaining objects are "filled in." There are several

Valence[a] (Cr/C)	Comments	Remarks & Observations
0/3		reinforces ends of C?
0/3		
0/3		
0/3		
0/1		
2/1		erases O1, redraws
4/3!	"Took care of me"	died
0/2		
0/2		
0/1		C incomplete
0/1		C incomplete
0/1		
0/1		C incomplete
0/2		C incomplete
0/2	•	
2/1		
3/2		
2/1		
4/1!		
4/1!		
3/1		

Time: 35 minutes

cousins, a few friends, roommates, and several girls with whom he had fleeting contact. All others are really acquaintances, couples he met, neighbors, and coworkers. Important are $O13$, his present boss, and $O15$, his supervisor. The supervisor advised him to seek treatment. The reason for this was $O16$, a coworker. "At work, whenever I turned around, this guy was sitting there. He was always staring at me. He was spreading the rumor that I was a queer." Objects 17 through 19 are young women who had rejected him, and objects 20 and 21 are former bosses whom he held responsible for having been fired from a previous job.

I asked the patient what the arrows at the ends of the connecting lines meant. He explained that they showed the direction of influence.

Scoring Sheet 7-8
Time: 35 minutes

A. Impressions

1. *Gestalt*   looks like a needle cushion
2. *Feeling tone*
    (alive–dead; friendly–angry)   dead and angry in controlled way
3. *Space and Distance*
    (full–empty; close–far)   full at core, otherwise empty; very close
4. *Differentiation and*
    Sophistication
    (primitive–sophisticated)   primitive
5. *Orderliness*
    (orderly–disorderly; calm–   orderly, mechanical; very controlled,
    wild)   but not calm
6. *Openness* (open–closed)   closed
7. *Symbolisms*   arrows

B. Variables

---

1. *Objects*
    Number   34
    Nature *(P/I/Th)*   34/0/0
    Form   Labels only
    Placement   bunched around "self," no discernible group-
                                    ing
    Sequence   Present girlfriend, family, work and its prob-
                                    lems, girls who "rejected him"
2. *Connecting lines (C)*   50, all with arrows, and 16 "incomplete"
3. *Crossbars (Cr)*   27
4. *Bond Index (C/O)*   1.47
5. *Separation Index (Cr/C)*   0.54
6. *Ratio C/O:Cr/C*   3:1
7. *Valences*   see protocol
8. *Distribution patterns*

C	0	1	2	3	more	Total
O	—	23	6	5	—	34

Cr	0	1	2	3	more	Total
O	25	—	3	3	3(all 4)	34

9. *Mean Distance (MD)*   3.4 cm
10. *Mean Difference in Distance*
    (MDD)   0.8 cm
11. *Ratio MDD:MD*   1/4
12. *Vollgestalt*   6
13. *Praegnanz*   3
14. *Percent of Symbolisms*   ?
15. *Order*   regular, *Cr* often delayed

COMMENT

Both these models show signs of depression, and—especially *Example 7-8*—of obsessional tendencies. They were selected, however, because of the excessive use of crossbars, and the addition of arrows to the connecting lines.

"Many" crossbars indicate definite separations and losses. At which point "many" becomes "too many," is difficult to say. One would certainly assume that there are too many crossbars in a model when they begin to outweigh the connecting lines. In *Example 7-7*, there are twice as many crossbars as there are connecting lines. We also know that the patient drew them with active intent—"when you quit, you quit!"—that they came in two bursts, and that he was preoccupied with death. While there can be no doubt that he was depressed, these other factors speak for a strong, underlying aggression, which breaks through. The best formulation might be: depressed mood with aggression controlled—triggered by association it bursts out, turns into vengeance (too many *Cr*), becomes controlled again, and ends in depression.

In *Example 7-8*, we have an entirely different picture. There are 27 *Cr*, giving a separation index of 0.54, and in three instances more than three *Cr* are assigned to one *O*. This pattern may still be within normal range. However, the invention of arrows makes the connecting lines look like darts. The patient's claim that these arrows indicate the direction of influence is not convincing. Any important relationship carries the notion of influence, but only one or two other subjects raised the question of its direction.* I would like to suggest that the arrows might have two meanings:

1. The patient is correct. They show the direction of influence. But influence is of such importance to him because he is afraid of being influenced, that is, they show his paranoid tendency.
2. The arrows turn every connecting line into a dart, one- or double-ended. Thus, the whole picture comes to look like a ball of clenched aggression—an impression which is only partially offset by the model's neatness and order.

* At one point, I became interest in the direction of connecting lines, and observed how they were drawn: toward the object, or toward the "self." If there is meaning to this difference, I was not able to discern it, because the direction of the connecting lines seemed to be mostly determined by habit and convenience. Apparently people find it easier to draw a straight line from left to right and downwards, rather than in the opposite directions, and thus connecting lines in the right half and lower part of the sheet were drawn toward the objects, and in the left half and the upper portion of the sheet toward the "self." Some subjects kept the sheet turning as they progressed, and drew all their lines toward the objects.

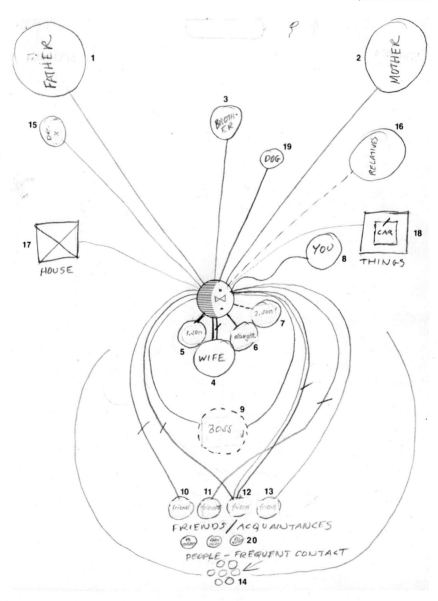

BORDERLINE

The term borderline, as it is being used here, connotes ego weakness, a distant, rather schizoid way of viewing the world, numerous ill-defined symptoms, and a readiness to react with incapacitating anxiety.

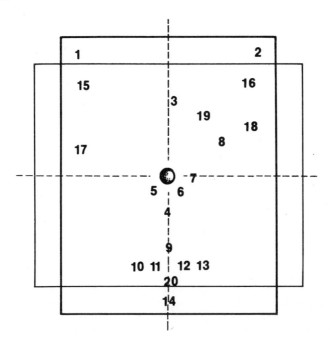

Example 7-9

The patient was in his forties, married, and had three children. His relationships were tenuous and dependent. He was able to hold a job, mostly because his boss was protective and tolerated frequent absences. While the patient was thus able to provide financially, he relied heavily on his wife in all other respects. His contact with friends, and even with his children, was very limited.

The patient had been in treatment previously but did not feel that he had been helped. When I began to see him, he suffered from multiple symptoms, all vague and shifting. He was anxious, phobic to the point of paralysis, and depressed. He was also often tired, and at such times presented somatic complaints. His capacity for insight was limited.

Clinical diagnosis: Borderline, schizoid character. (See Fig. 7-9 and Protocol 7-9.)

Protocol 7-9

Order & Sequence (O,C,Cr,L)	Object[a]	Placement	
		Distance[a]	Location
O1 . . .	Erased		8
O1,C1(1),L1	Father	12.5	11
O2,C2(1),L2	Mother	13	1
O3,C3(1),L3	Brother	8	12
O4,O5,O6,O7,L4,L5,L6, ⎫	Wife	2	6
L7,C5(1),C6(1),C7(1?) ⎬	1st son	1.5	7
	2nd son	2	4
C4(1),Cr4(1) ⎭	Daughter	1.5	5
O8,L8,C8(1)	Therapist	5	2
O9,L9,C9(2)	Boss	5.5	6
O10,O11,O12, . . . ⎫	Friends	10	6
O13,L10,L11,L12,L13, ⎬		9.5	
C10(1),C11(1),C12(3),C13(1)		9.5	
Cr10(1),Cr11(1),Cr12(2) ⎭		10	
O14,L14, . . .,C14(2)	People	13	6
O15,L15, . . .,C15(1)	Former therapist	11	11
O16,L16, . . .,C16(1)	Relatives	9	2
O17,L17,C17(1)	House	7	10
O18,L18,C18(1)	Car, things	7.5	2
O19,L19,C19(1)	Dog	7	1
O20,L20, . . .,C4(1)	Acquaintances	11	6

[a] Filled in after completion of test.

SUMMARY OF OBSERVATIONS AND INTERVIEW

It took this patient an inordinately long time to complete the test. In fact, he stopped because the hour was up. Responsible was his inability to decide. He accompanied his work with running comments. To begin with, he talked about the "self": "This is an eclipse of the moon . . . no, I should be logical, it is a ball . . . or a hole with depth. . . . how am I to connect people to this?. . . right away you throw me into a graphic problem. . . . Should I draw this literally?. . . maybe it's a man with a beard. Boy, this is tough!. . . . I am not supposed to complete me?" Whereupon he drew a face into the "self." He could not decide how to

Valence[a] (Cr/C)	Comments	Remarks & Observations
	"Eclipse of moon". . . "No, ball . . .	Very anxious, turns card,
	a hole . . . a man with beard . . ."	takes 5 minutes to start.
		Begins by drawing eyes
		and nose in "self"
0/1		
0/1		
0/1		
1/2		
0/1	"Girl sort of in between"	erases, redraws O6,
0/1?		delays!
0/1		
0/1	"Where do I go from that? . . .	wavy C,
	You, out here"	
0/2	"I'm not sure of him"	turns card
1/1	"Friends . . . I don't have any	
	anymore"	erases, redraws closer
1/1		
2/3		waits
0/1		
0/2		C incomplete . . . waits . . .
0/1	"I ought to put him in"	. . . waits . . .
0/1?		C dotted
1/1		cross in house
1/1		Cr into O18
0/1		
0/0		No C! 2nd C for wife
	Time: 50 minutes	

begin for several more minutes. Finally, he made up his mind to "put them all in and then see what they are."

The first three objects were his father, mother, and brother. He changed the father's location twice, and rearranged the label for the mother. In placing his present family he first lined up the objects, then the labels, erased and rearranged them, and finally put in the connecting lines. But only one per person. The second connecting line for his wife was added at the end of the test. His boss (O9) has a dotted boundary because "I am not sure of him." The friends (O10–13) are there because "they once were my friends." He was not sure whether to represent them as a group called "friends," or singly and give them their real names. Eventually he decided for the latter. Probably without being aware of it, he connected one of these friends (O12) with three lines, the only person to be so strongly attached. When I asked him about that later, he could not explain it. There was nothing special about this relationship.

Object 8, the therapist, received a wavy line because "the relationship is not direct. I am coming and going." The previous therapist (O15) was placed close to his father because "up there are the child relationships." The patient invented his own version of interruption for O17 (house) and O18 (car-things). He put a cross inside the house "because I liked it, and I hated it," and the crossbar for the car into the boundary of the object "because the car is no longer the same." (Is it damaged? body image?). House and car-things are represented as squares "because things are things. They have sharp edges . . . you put in a lot of expense, effort and money." Towards the end of the test, the patient added the family dog (O19), and relatives and acquaintances (O16 and O20). The latter have no connecting lines.

Scoring Sheet 7-9
Time: 50 minutes

A.	Impressions	
1.	*Gestalt*	
2.	*Feeling tone* (alive–dead; friendly–angry)	not dead but empty, lots of hollow spaces; rather bland, not warm
3.	*Space and Distance* (full–empty; close–far)	not full, not empty; very close and very far
4.	*Differentiation and Sophistication* (primitive–sophisticated)	I opt for primitive because of the patient's profession
5.	*Orderliness* (orderly–discorderly; calm–wild)	definite attempts at organization; it is strange, a little weird
6.	*Openness* (open–closed)	not really open, despite the open spaces
7.	*Symbolisms*	face in "self," dotted lines and boundaries, the womb-like configuration of the C in the lower part, the squareness of house and things

B.	Variables	
1.	*Objects* Number	20

	Nature *(P/I/Th)*	18/0/2
	Form	circles and squares
	Placement	in regions and groups
	Sequence	Original family, present family, therapist, work, distant people, things
2.	*Connecting lines (C)*	25
3.	*Crossbars (Cr)*	7 (2 variations)
4.	*Bond Index (C/O)*	1.25 low
5.	*Separation Index (Cr/C)*	0.28
6.	*Ratio C/O:Cr/C*	5:1
7.	*Valences*	see protocol

8. *Distribution patterns*

C	0	1	2	3	more	Total
O	1	15	3	1	—	20

Cr	0	1	2	3	more	Total
O	14	5	1	—	—	20

9.	*Mean Distance (MD)*	7.8 cm, rather far
10.	*Mean Difference in Distance (MDD)*	3.1 cm
11.	*Ratio MDD:MD*	1/2.5
12.	*Vollgestalt*	5
13.	*Praegnanz*	3
14.	*Percent of Symbolisms*	about 20%
15.	*Order*	frequent delays: *O, L,* and *C* in sequences, *Cr* delayed

EVALUATION AND COMMENT

One could ask why this patient should not be considered psychotic. Clinical impressions, some of his comments, and several features of the test might warrant such a diagnosis. I opted for borderline because in some important respects the patient still functioned fairly well, and his test showed a certain stability and order. I shall describe those features which I believe to be indicative of a loosening of thinking and boundaries. We will find these features even more evident in the models of psychotics.

The test is a good example of the struggle between compulsive defenses, which attempt to retain form and contact, and primitive elements, which force their way through.

There are the symbolisms, including the uterus-like shape of the lower connecting lines; the uncertainty about attachments and separations, which led to many delays and corrections; and the beginning confusion about boundaries (in *O*9, *O*17 and *O*18). The bond index is low, that is, relationships are experienced as weak. In the distribution pattern, we see that all relationships are of this kind, except one (which, incongruously, is indicated as strong).

We also find "things" in this model. "Things" are extremely rare for adults. One could argue that they should be scored as "ideas." That would have been my inclination, except that the patient himself called them things, and treated them as such. I believe that these "things" could be considered transitional objects, in the same way as in the models of adolescent patients. Their placement might support such an assumption. If one looks at the general distribution of objects, it becomes apparent that the patient divided the sheet into regions. Between 11 and 2 o'clock, and far out, he placed his childhood; at 10 and 2 o'clock he put the "things"; and into the lower portion he drew his present family, his relationships at work, friends, and people. The form of the connecting lines underscores this division: They radiate in the upper half, and they bend and enclose in the lower. In other words, he stratified the sheet into the distant past, the more recent past, and the present.

PSYCHOSIS

The following two models were done by psychotic patients.

Example 7-10

Example 7-10 is the work of a chronic schizophrenic. The patient was a bright, college-educated woman in her forties who had five children. Her husband provided a comfortable income, and was in general supportive. The patient's illness became evident following the birth of her first child. She had spent many years in psychotherapy with several psychiatrists, and had, to some degree, been helped. Hospitalization was never necessary.

Some ten years before her present therapy, the patient converted to Catholicism. Her faith was of paramount importance, and was used by her in a supportive as well as a defensive way. She had many contacts with the church, which she shifted according to need, and occasionally developed religious delusions. (See Fig. 7-10 and Protocol 7-10.)

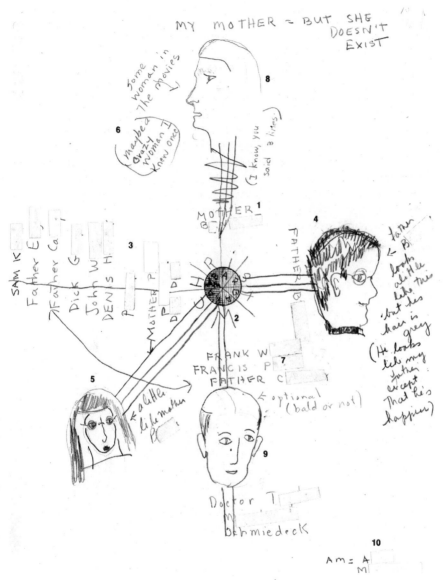

Figure 7-10

143

SUMMARY OF OBSERVATIONS AND INTERVIEW

There was a great deal of hesitation, erasing, and redrawing. The patient's first step was to darken the area of the "self" and draw crosses into it. In the next step, she drew her name inside, and also her initials. She explained that the crosses were a mandala. At the end of the test she repeated her initials in the lower, right corner ($O10$), and also spelled out her full names. These are three confirmations of her identity!

Object 1 is the mother superior of a convent the patient frequently visits; $O2$ is Christ, spelled out around the "self"—the M stands for "our lady, Mary"; $O3$ is "really a list of friends"; and $O4$ is a priest "who was always there and abstaining." Object 5 is another nun, $O6$ is self-explanatory, and $O7$ is three more friends. Then she drew her mother ($O8$) on top, and in profile. The mother's eyes were erased and redrawn. The comment reads, "I know you said three lines." These three lines were crossed out (angrily). It is difficult to translate this zig-zag line into crossbars, but it would seem to stand for several. Object 9 is three physicians who treated her. The present therapist is the last. I asked if she

Protocol 7-10

Order & Sequence (O,C,Cr,L)	Object[a]	Placement Distance[a]	Location
$L1,C1(1)$	Mother B	3	12
$L2$,no $C!$	Christ & M	1?	around "self"
$L3,C3(1)$	List of names	2.5–10	9
$O4,L4,C4(3)$	Father B.	4	3
$O5,L5,C5(3)$	Mother P.	8	7
$L6$, no $C!$	Crazy woman	6.5	11
$L7$, no $C!$	3 names	3.5	6
$O8,L8,C8(3),Cr8?$	Mother	7	12
$O9,C9(2),L9$	3 psychiatrists	10–12	6
$L10$, no $C!$	Her initials	14	5

Omissions: father, stepfather, siblings, husband, children

[a] Filled in after completion of test.

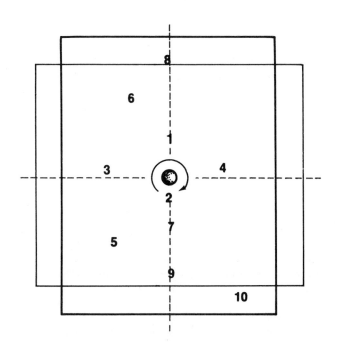

Valence[a] (Cr/C)	Comments	Remarks & Observations
	"What if I feel nobody is important?"	turns card, shades light part of "self," then darkens darker part. Puts 2 crosses into it. Puts her name in —then, separately her initials.
	"I wrote my name in there"	
0/1		
0/0!		
0/1		
0/3		
0/3		
0/0!		
0/0!		
?/3?		*C* incomplete *Cr* as ∼∼∼∼∼
0/2		*C* right through *L*7
0/0!		adds comment to *O*4
		a good deal of erasing and redrawing throughout

Time: 31 minutes

forgot anyone, in particular her husband and children. Her answer was: "I didn't feel like putting them in. You asked who affected me, not how I affected them." She also explained the mandala: "It's a symbol of the soul, of creation. That's what happens at conception."

Scoring Sheet 7-10
Time: 31 minutes

A.	Impressions	
1.	*Gestalt*	strange, disturbed design
2.	*Feeling tone* (alive–dead; friendly–angry)	this picture is alive, with a mixture of feelings, some startling
3.	*Space and Distance* (full–empty; close–far)	fairly full, and rather far as far as people are concerned
4.	*Differentiation and Sophistication* (primitive–sophisticated)	both, mixed
5.	*Orderliness* (orderly–disorderly; calm–wild)	not well ordered, but not disorganized, very mixed
6.	*Openness* (open–closed)	rather closed
7.	*Symbolisms*	several, drawn at the beginning of the test

B.	Variables	
1.	*Objects*	
	Number	10
	Nature *(P/I/Th)*	7/3/0[a] I% = 30
	Form	labels, faces, comments, mixed
	Placement	mixed, did she still follow the cross?
	Sequence	Her own name, religion, friends, religion, the crazy woman, friends, mother, therapists, herself
2.	*Connecting lines (C)*	13 (but 4O without C; the 3C to O8 fade into the 1C of O1)
3.	*Crossbars (Cr)*	0.0 (the break with O8 is definite though)
4.	*Bond Index (C/O)*	1.3 low (for the 7 "people" = 1.86)
5.	*Separation Index (Cr/C)*	0.0, cannot be established
6.	*Ratio (C/O:Cr/C)*	1.3:0

7. *Valences*   see protocol
8. *Distribution patterns*

C	0	1	2	3	more	Total
O	4!	2	1	3	—	10

Cr	0	1	2	3	more	Total
O	9	—	—	1?	—	10

9. *Mean Distance (MD)*   difficult to establish, around 6.5 cm
10. *Mean Difference in Distance*
    (MDD)   about 3.0 cm
11. *Ratio MDD:MD*   1/2
12. *Vollgestalt*   5
13. *Praegnanz*   0
14. *Percent of Symbolisms*   fairly high, but not too high—probably 30%
15. *Order*   The end product looks limited but fairly regular. The process was quite irregular, with much erasing, redrawing and delaying

---

[a] There are actually many more "people" in this test, but only four are specified. The others are listed, not individualized. Her relationship to them remains vague. The confirmations of the patient's identity and the "crazy woman" are counted as "ideas," since they refer to concerns about herself.

Example 7-11

Model 7-11 was done by a single, 30-year-old East-Indian engineer. He came from a large-well-established family, and apparently was the only child who had not done very well. When I met him, he had been living and working with a group of American friends, whom he eagerly emulated. He presented himself as a hard-driving, all-American executive who had forgotten his past. In fact, he was a man without anchorage.

Following the death of a famous figure on the American business scene, the patient became delusional. He identified with this man, drove himself in restless but ineffectual activity, and developed mathematical systems which dealt with success and the meaning of life.

The patient was hospitalized twice, the first time during a manic phase, the second time with a deep depression. The test was taken shortly after the first hospitalization.

Clinical diagnosis: Manic-depressive psychosis. (See Fig. 7-11 and Protocol 7-11.)

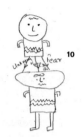

1 father ≡ } back
2 Mother ≡ } home
3 family ≡ }

4 K ♀ ⊯ uncertain (1)
5 E ♀ # past (X)
6 J ♂ ≠ (5)
7 B ♂ ≡ (4) America
8 P ♂ ≡ (2)
9 H ♂ ≡ (3)

10

Protocol 7-11

Order & Sequence (O,C,Cr,L)	Object[a]	Placement Distance[a]	Location
	Patient starts off with a list in upper left corner. Having finished it, he draws O10.		
L1	Father	16	11
L2	Mother	15	11
L3	Family	14	11
L4	Girlfriend	14	10
L5	Ex-girlfriend	13	10
L6	Roommate	13	10
L7	Friend	13	10
L8	Boss	13	10
L9	Friend	12	9
O10,L10	Fear, uncertainty, unknown	8	2

[a] Filled in after completion of test.

148

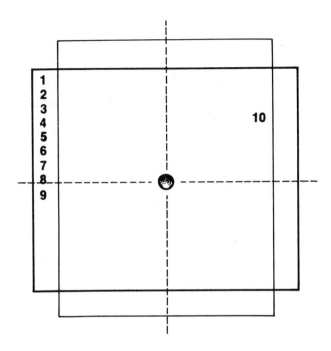

Valence[a] (Cr/C)	Comments	Remarks & Observations
(0/3)		
(0/3)		
(0/3)		
(1/3)		
(3/3)		
(1/3)		
(0/3)		
(0/3)		
(0/3)		

Time: 6 minutes

SUMMARY OF OBSERVATIONS AND INTERVIEW

The patient began with a list of labels in the upper left corner. Apparently this was an attempt at control. The list contains his parents and his family, that is, all his siblings and relatives lumped together (O1–3), followed by his American friends. When I pointed out that he had not connected anyone to himself, he said that he had not paid attention, and proceeded to rank his friends in order of importance (numbers in brackets). Object 4 is his present girlfriend, O8 his boss, and O9 is the one friend whom he might actually trust. By this I mean that the patient expects him to act rationally in response to his illness. All other friends he does not consider reliable. They busy themselves around him, but their efforts hinder rather than help his treatment.

Object 10 seems to be the patient himself and his illness. The upper figure has three legs; he explained: "I came up with a three-legged problem (fear, uncertainty, unknown). I want to go back."

Scoring Sheet 7-11
Time: 6 minutes

A.	Impressions	
1.	*Gestalt*	clearly unusual, no coherence or real Gestalt
2.	*Feeling tone* (alive–dead; friendly–angry)	helpless, strange, surprising, even some humor(O10), totally disconnected
3.	*Space and Distance* (full–empty; close–far)	empty and far
4.	*Differentiation and Sophistication* (primitive–sophisticated)	really neither
5.	*Orderliness* (orderly–disorderly; calm–wild)	orderly, attempt at structuring; looks calm but is not
6.	*Openness* (open–closed)	totally open
7.	*Symbolisms*	O10

B.	Variables	
1.	*Objects*	
	Number	10
	Nature *(P/I/Th)*	9/1/0
	Form	list of labels, one drawing
	Placement	left and right, upper half
	Sequence	Family, friends, psychosis
2.	*Connecting lines (C)*	0, or 27 very "incomplete" C
3.	*Crossbars (Cr)*	0, or 5

4.	*Bond Index (C/O)*	0.0, or 2.7, or for "people" 3.0
5.	*Separation Index (Cr/C)*	0.0, or 0.18
7.	*Valences*	none, or all with 3C, except what is his illness or he himself

8. *Distribution patterns*

C	0	1	2	3	more	Total
O		10	(or 9 with 3 "incomplete" C each)			

Cr	0	1	2	3	more	Total
O		10	—	—	—	—	10
or						
		7	2	—	1	—	10

9.	*Mean Distance (MD)*	(to labels and figures) 13.0 cm
10.	*Mean Difference in Distance (MDD)*	meaningless
12.	*Vollgestalt*	2
13.	*Praegnanz*	0
14.	*Percent of Symbolisms*	?
15.	*Order*	only vestiges of regularity

EVALUATIONS AND COMMENT

These tests were difficult to score. This is typical for the models of psychotics. Their treatment of the test elements is so ambiguous that one cannot be sure of assigning accurate values. It is this very ambiguity, though, the scattering of regular and irregular responses, mixed with innovations, which reflects the patient's inability to use the instructions and form stable conceptualizations.

If we examine the protocol and the scoring sheet of *Example 7-10*, it becomes obvious how conventional representation is followed by fantastic elaboration; how form, context, and relationships fluctuate between the concrete and the vague; and how elusive some of the patient's meanings are. The model is not orderly, but also not disorderly; it is, perhaps, angry, and certainly not dead; connections are there and not there; sophisticated and primitive elements are intermingled. There is no way in which all of this can be put together into an integrated whole.

In *Example 7-11*, the disintegration is even more evident. There are, strictly counting, ten objects, but really only two messages. The patient is totally disconnected, and he is torn apart by fear and uncertainty. One might interpret the figure (O10) in this model in several other ways, but its essential meaning will remain the same.

The list of names is orderly, organized, and neat. He is an engineer, and this is his attempt to approach the problem methodically. But the effort leads nowhere. It remains, literally, "out in the left field." There is very little one can do with the variables. Their values are ambiguous or even obscure.

The question might be raised: Did the patient indeed not pay attention? I think he did, or at least tried, but was confused and disorganized and unable to put the whole thing together.

REVERSE SIDE

The following two models illustrate a rare but interesting variation. The subjects, after completing the test on one side, turned the sheet over and continued on the reverse side. Their "backside" models are less controlled, and show a more intimate and fantastic content. The information accompanying these examples is limited to data which are relevant for the difference between front- and backside.

Example 7-12

This model was drawn by a middle-aged man who was mildly depressed. His main conflict centered around the separation from his wife—and separations in general. (See Fig. 7-12.)

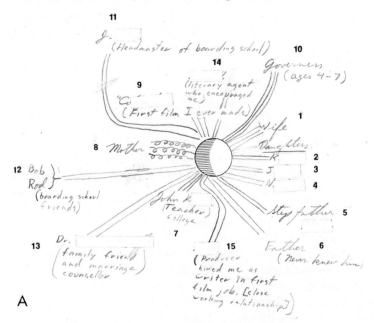

Figure 7-12*A* and *B*. *B* is the reverse side of *A*.

There is not much difference between the two sides. The character of the Gestalt is very similar, though on the reverse side the Gestalt is a little larger. There are 15 objects in front and 10 in back; the bond index of the backside is slightly lower (2.0 vs 2.33); neither side contains crossbars.

But the backside is marked by an awkwardly smiling face in the "self," and in general seems to be closer to his feelings. The patient wrote a good many explanations into his test; on the backside they become more extensive. In front he deals with history: his background, education, work, and present family. On the reverse side he turns to conflicts, loves, and hopes—several objects seem to represent facets of himself. They have talent but are immature, make mistakes, and are not appreciative.

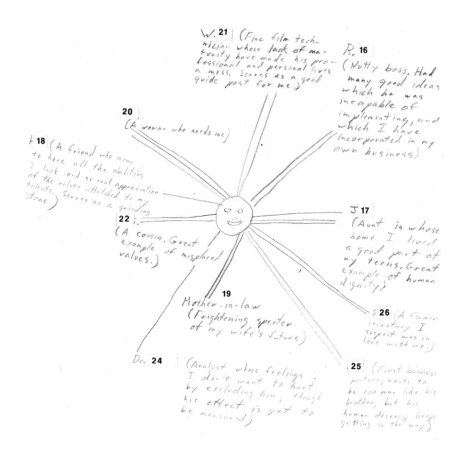

B

Three objects are concerned with love, in the past, present, and future. And there is the therapist, whom he does not yet know but does not wish to offend.

Example 7-13

This model was drawn by an 18-year-old girl. She had been adopted, and was in treatment because she could not function in college. (See Fig. 7-13.)

The test has many interesting features. It contains only few relationships that are not conflicted or broken off, a great deal of fantasy, and a conglomeration or fusion of objects. The clinical diagnosis was borderline state.

Important for our purposes is the difference between front and back. Both sides are again similar, but the frontside is better organized. Placements and sequence are fairly clear; there are connecting lines and interruptions, and while primary processes intrude, the patient always returns to reality and the task at hand. On the reverse side this is no longer so. The drawings flow into each other, placement is diffuse, and there are no longer any connections and separations. We have, as it were, entered the patient's world of memory and fantasy.

It is worthwhile to describe some of the "backside" objects: $O19$ is spread over the upper half of the sheet. It is a friend of the patient's mother, in her garden, close to her house. The drawing relates to early childhood experiences. Object 22 is "me," the patient herself. Object 23 is a ballet dancer. This is the patient's real mother—or rather, this is all she knows about her real mother. Object 21, the drummerboy, and $O24$, the elephant, are childhood toys. They are transitional objects in the original sense of the term.

TESTS AND RETESTS

At the conclusion of this chapter, a short series of tests and retests is presented. The examples are rather typical and demonstrate two important aspects: (1) Certain variables, primarily the Gestalt, show very little change from test to retest. (2) Changes, which are clinically apparent, are reflected in the retests. They are not necessarily obvious, but become evident when one analyzes the data.

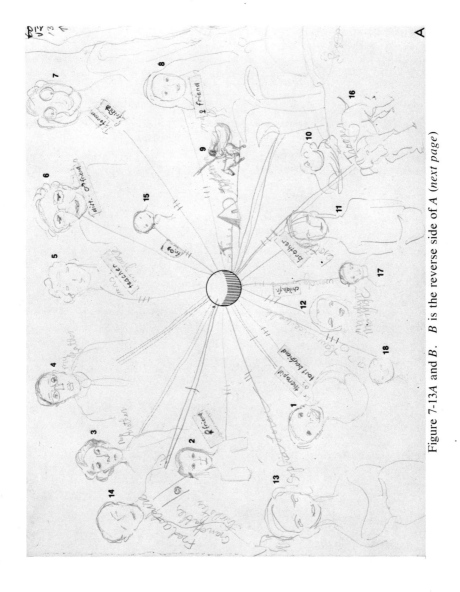

Figure 7-13A and B. B is the reverse side of A (next page)

155

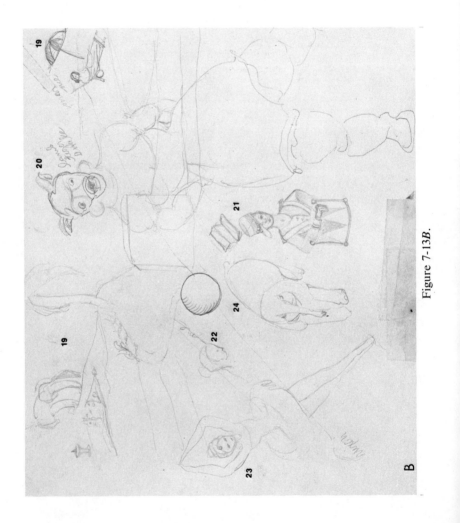

Figure 7-13*B*.

156

EXAMPLES 7-14A AND 7-14B (INTERVAL—32 MONTHS)

These two models were drawn by a middle-aged man who entered treatment because of marital and sexual difficulties. He was mildly depressed, and expected direct support. Treatment did not improve his marriage, but did enable him to feel and express anger, and to become more independent. (See Fig. 7-14.)

Test and retest look similar. They have the same basic Gestalt, and they are simple, bland and rather unimaginative. The Gestalt of the retest is fuller and larger, and its contour less rigid.

The number of objects grew from nine to 19, but this increase was accomplished entirely through the addition of "ideas." They have to do with his work and his worries. He has established a (ambivalent) relationship with the therapist, and is concerned with the outcome of treatment, and with the future (Objects 15, 16, 18, and 19).

It remains questionable whether relationships on the whole have improved. The bond index increased; the separation index remained the same. But this needs to be qualified: The bond index for "people only,"

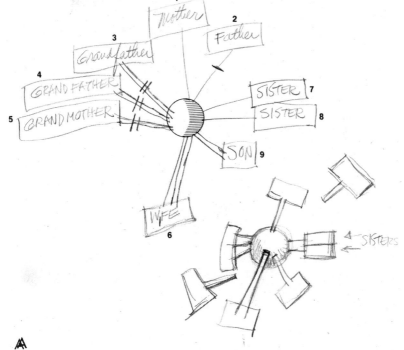

Figure 7-14A and B.   The smaller design in the lower right corner was added after completion of the design. The patient wanted to show how his model would look if it were three-dimensional. (B on next page.)

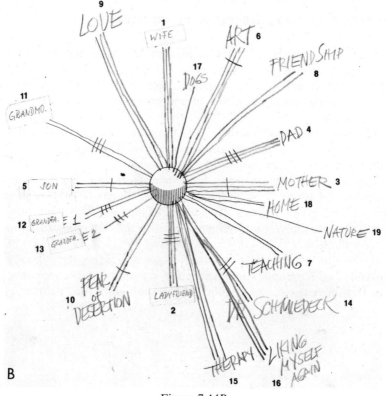

Figure 7-14*B*.

that is, the nine "people" in the retest (not counting the dog), is 2.3. But
the separation index for "people only" is 0.9, which is very high. I am
inclined to say that this reflects his anger, and that he has become, if not
warmer, at least more alive in his relationships.

EXAMPLES 7-15A AND 7-15B (INTERVAL—NINE MONTHS)

This patient, a young, single woman, had lost her mother shortly
before entering treatment. Her father had died when she was a child. The
remaining relatives, one brother and an aunt and her family, are in the
tests. She was bitter, isolated, and depressed, and suffered from migraine.
(See Fig. 7-15.)

The Gestalt on test and retest is congruent. The design has been tilted
upward on the retest. It is smaller, more abstract, and more controlled,
but has retained its basic character and contour.

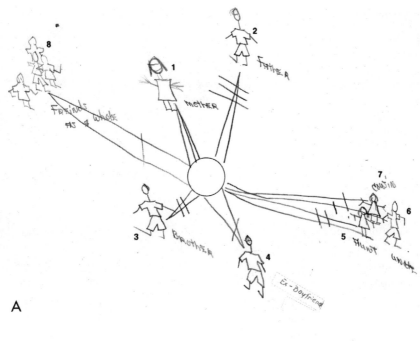

A

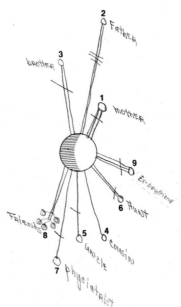

B

Figure 7-15*A* and *B*.

Summary of Scoring Sheets for Examples 7-14A and 7-14B

		Test	Retest
Objects	No.:	9	19
Nature	(P/I/Th):	9/0/0	10/9/0
Form:		boxes & labels	labels
Placement:		wheel	wheel
Sequence and Composition:			present family shifted forward, parents and grandparents back; sisters dropped, "Ideas" and therapist added.
C:		15	43
Cr:		7	21
Bond Index (C/O):		1.7	2.3 ("people only": 2.3)
Separation Index (Cr/C):		0.46	0.49 ("people only": 0.9)
C/O:Cr/C:		3.7:1	4.7:1

Valences and Distances:

	Cr/C	cm	Cr/C	cm
Mother	0/1	4	1/3	5
Father	1/1	4	3/3	6
Grandfather 1	2/2	4	3/2	4.5
Grandfather 2	2/2	3.5	3/1	3.5
Grandmother	2/2	3	3/2	7
Wife	0/3	4	0/3	7
Son	0/2	2.5	1/2	4.5
Woman friend	—	—	3/3	5
Art	—	—	1/3	5
Teaching	—	—	0/2	6.5
Friendship	—	—	0/2	8.5
Love	—	—	0/3	8
Fear of Desertion	—	—	1/2	6
Therapist	—	—	2/2	7
Therapy	—	—	0/3	9
Like myself	—	—	0/3	10
Dogs	—	—	0/1	5
Home	—	—	0/2	5
Nature	—	—	0/1	8

Distribution patterns:

	C	0	1	2	3	more	Total
T	O	—	4	4	1	—	15
RT	O	—	3	8	8	—	43
"people only" RT	O	—	1	4	4	—	21

Cr	0	1	2	3	more	Total
T O	5	1	3	—	—	7
RT O	9	4	1	5	—	21
"people only" RT O	1	2	1	5	—	19

	Test	Retest
MD:	3.5	6.5
MDD:	0.4	1.5
MDD:MD:	1/9	1/4
Vollgestalt:	5	6
Praegnanz:	3	3
Symbol %:	0	0
Order:	regular	regular

Summary of Scoring Sheets for Examples 7-15A and 7-15B

		Test		Retest	
Objects	No.:	8		9	
Nature	(P/I/Th):	8/0/0		9/0/0	
Form:		stick figures		circles	
Placement:		star		star	
Sequence &				hardly changed. Ex-boyfriend	
Composition:				moved to end, therapist added	
C:		15		17	
Cr:		11		9	
Bond Index (C/O):		1.87		1.88	
Separation Index (Cr/C):		0.73		0.53	
C/O:Cr/C:	`	2.6:1		3.5:1	
Valences and Distances:		Cr/C	cm	Cr/C	cm
	Mother	0/3	4	1/3	2.5
	Father	3/2	5.5	3/2	6.5
	Brother	2/2	3	1/2	4
	Ex-boyfriend	1/2	4	1/3	3
	Aunt	2/2	8	1/2	3
	Uncle	1/1	9	1/1	4
	Cousin	1/1	8	0/1	4.5
	Friends	1/2	9	0/2	3.5
	Therapist	—	—	1/1	5.5

Distribution patterns:

C	0	1	2	3	more	Total
T O	—	2	5	1	—	15
RT O	—	3	4	2	—	17

Cr	0	1	2	3	more	Total
T O	1	4	2	1	—	11
RT O	2	6	—	1	—	9

	Test	*Retest*
MD:	5.9	4.2
MDD:	2.25	1.0
MDD:MD:	1/3	1/4
Vollgestalt:	4	3
Praegnanz:	3	5
Symbol %:	0	0
Order:	regular	regular

Some of the variables also remained surprisingly unchanged: The number of objects, their nature, the bond index, and the composition and sequence of objects, are the same or nearly the same. Two changes—the decrease in the mean difference in distance and the increase in Praegnanz—speak for even greater rigidity. On the other hand, there are also positive changes: The separation index dropped and the mean distance decreased, that is, all objects moved closer. Exceptions are the patient's dead father and her brother, who were placed at greater distance. A similar movement becomes apparent in the valences, which show fewer crossbars and greater variation in the number of bonds.

EXAMPLES 7-16A AND 7-16B (INTERVAL—25 MONTHS)

The last two models in this series are from an artistically gifted woman. They illustrate how emotional changes are reflected in the drawings themselves, while much of the basic form and Gestalt of the tests remain unchanged.

When first tested, the patient had just gone through a divorce. She was determined to make it on her own. She suppressed many of her feelings and minimized the difficulties of life as a single woman. By the time of the second test, she had suffered several disappointments and setbacks. She was still quite constricted emotionally, but more realistic and much angrier. (See Fig. 7-16.)

Gestalt and groupings have been largely retained, but the overall impression has changed. The figures on the test are neatly and carefully drawn, they are clearly recognizable, and there is a distinct sense of order. On the retest the figures have become haphazard and less distinct, but at the same time more expressive. The overall sense has changed to upset and anger.

At first sight, many of the variables look unchanged, much as we have seen in the two preceding examples. However, this is not really so: The number of objects remained nearly the same, but there are fewer "people" in the retest, and instead four "ideas" which are obviously problematic and painful. Form and placement remained very similar, and so did the sequence. Merely father and mother, and boyfriend and ex-husband, changed positions. The bond index is exactly the same for both tests, the separation index dramatically increased. But again, this might be misleading. If we look at "people only," we find that the bond index has become stronger, and the separation index slightly weaker. In other

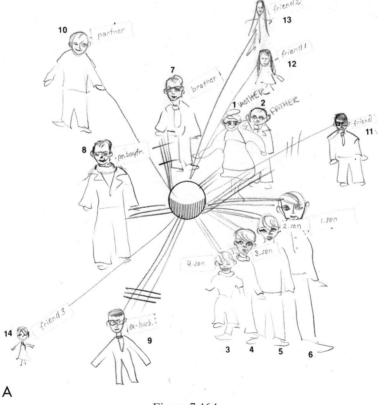

A

Figure 7-16A.

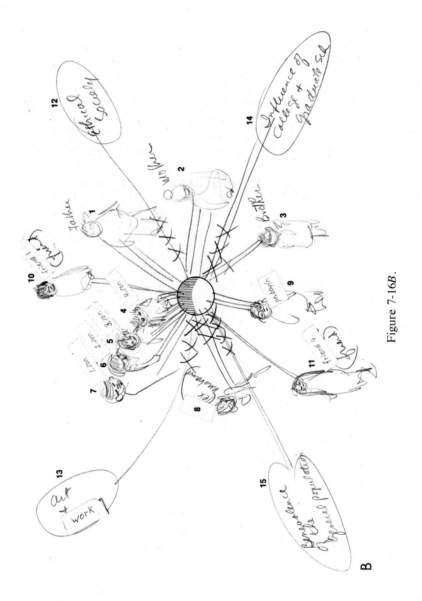

Figure 7-16*B*.

words, the attachment to "people" seems to have become more intense. The results for the mean distance repeat this pattern. The values for all objects are the same, but the "people" have been drawn closer.

In summary, the patient appears more upset and angry on the retest, but also more aware of her problems. Her circle of "people" has narrowed. She has stronger feelings for them, and probably a greater need to remain attached.

Summary of Scoring Sheet for Examples 7-16A and 7-16B

		Test		Retest	
Objects	No.:	14		15	
Nature	*(P/I/Th):*	14/0/0		11/4/0	
Form:		figures		figures and labels	
Placement:				very similar, some shifts of individual positions[a]	
Sequence and Composition:				nearly the same, father–mother, and ex-husband–present boyfriend changed positions, four "people" are dropped, one added, four "ideas" added.	
C:		32		35	
Cr:		8		32 (16)[a]	
Bond Index	*(C/O):*	2.3		2.3 ("people only": 2.6)	
Separation Index (Cr/C):		0.25		0.9 ("people only": 0.2)	
C/O:Cr/C:		9:1		2.5:1	
Valences and Distances:		*Cr/C*	*cm*	*Cr/C*	*cm*
	Mother	0/3	2	0/3	4
	Father	0/3	4	0/3	4
	4. Son	0/3	3	0/3	1.5
	3. Son	0/3	3	0/3	2
	2. Son	0/3	4	0/3	3
	1. Son	0/3	5	0/3	4
	Brother	2/3	3	2/2	4
	Present boyfriend	0/3	3	0/3	3
	Ex-husband	3/3	6	4/2	5
	Partner	0/1	7	—	—
	College friend	3/1	8	—	—
	Present girlfriend	0/1	8	0/2	4
	Present girlfriend 2	0/1	9	—	—
	Present girlfriend 3	0/1	10	—	—

Present girlfriend 4	—	—	0/2	6.5
Ethical society	—	—	6/1	9
Art and work	—	—	6/1	10
Influence of college and graduate school	—	—	6/2	9
Benevolence of the general population	—	—	8/2	9

Distribution patterns:

C	0	1	2	3	more	Total
T O	—	5	—	9	—	32
RT O	—	2	6	7	—	35
"people only" RT O	—	—	4	7	—	29

Cr	0	1	2	3	more	Total
T O	11	—	1	2	—	8
RT O	9	—	1	—	5 (30)	32
"people only" RT O	9	—	1	—	1 (4)	6

	Test	Retest
MD:	5.3	5.2 ("people only": 3.7)
MMDD:	2.2	2.3 ("people only": 1.7)
MDD:MD:	1/2.5	1/2.5
Vollgestalt:	6	6
Praegnanz:	2	1
Symbol %:	0	0
Order:	regular with some *Cr* delays	irregular, *O, L* first, the delayed *C* and *Cr* in blocks

[a] Two versions: 16 *Cr* if one counts only each cross, 32 *Cr* if one counts strictly, i.e., each cross consists of two crossbars. I opted for the second version.

With the above presentation of examples, the description of the personal sphere model has been concluded. The next two chapters will provide some further proof of validity and reliability, describe the application of the test to groups and to "normal" and foreign populations, and deal with theoretical aspects.

8
Application to Normal and Foreign Populations, and Other Studies

This chapter is devoted to the review of four independent investigations, which supplement and confirm our findings on reliability and validity, and show the applicability of the test in groups and non-American populations.

I shall first describe an early study, in which I attempted to correlate PSM results with demographic data, assuming that certain regularities could be found (Schmiedeck, 1971). The study was based on the models of 52 subjects and included the PSM variables: number of objects, bond index and separation-index; and the "life-cycle" variables: age, sex, marital status, family size (present and parental), number of children, religious background, education, and "intellectualism."

Religious background was defined as the religious atmosphere in which the subject grew up, and only secondarily as his present religious preference or involvement. For education, the sample was divided into college graduates and high school graduates. As it happened, the two groups were of equal size. "Intellectualism" was a composite variable. It was defined as a degree of sophistication, interest in intellectual or artistic pursuits and in books, and being informed; most important was the ability to make use of these pursuits in order to change ideas and attitudes. The variable was assessed on the basis of the examiner's impressions as a clinician and therapist, and had some connection with the extent of formal education. The rating was: Intellectualism-positive or -negative. Incidentally, the sample fell again into two equal parts.

The correlations were evaluated by comparing the means of the variables, and in scattergrams.

We found that the bond index and the separation index remained independent of the "life-cycle" variables, but that the number of objects was correlated.

Of all the "life-cycle" variables, age emerged as the single most important factor in determining the number of objects. Young people under twenty had the smallest range. After twenty, the number of objects grew steadily and reached its maximum in the age group of the 40- to 50-year-old. After fifty, the number of objects declined again. This finding applied to "all objects" and to "people" (it was, in fact, caused by an increase in the number of "people"). It did not apply to "ideas," which moved in the opposite direction. The number of "ideas" was relatively high in the models of the young and decreased with age.

Other "life-cycle" variables, such as marital status, size of the present family, and number of children, are themselves dependent on age. We found the largest object ranges in subjects who were married and had two or three children. Single subjects, or subjects with no children, had relatively narrow ranges. Unexpectedly, we also found small ranges in subjects with many children. The size of the parental family had no influence whatever on the number of objects.

Formal education and "intellectualism" also proved to have bearing. College graduates and subjects rated intellectualism-positive had wider object ranges (based on "people," not "ideas").

A surprising finding emerged in the correlation of object range and religious background: Jewish subjects showed a wide range (21 $O:$ 20 "people," 1 "idea"); Catholic subjects clustered close to the general median (16 $O:$ 12 "people," 4 "ideas"); and Protestant subjects fell slightly below this median (13 $O:$ 11 "people," 2 "ideas"). The difference 's evident for "people" and "ideas," but more impressive for "people." In search of an explanation, we cross-correlated religious background with the other "life-cycle" variables and found that some of them (e.g., age and family size) might have influenced the object range, but that this influence was slight and could not account for the variance. An attempt to correlate the object ranges with diagnostic criteria was also not conclusive.

The second study to be reviewed was conducted at the University of Vienna, in cooperation with Th. Kohlmann (Schmiedeck & Kohlmann, 1975). It was based on comparisons between clinical assessments and personal sphere models, and focused on the validity of the personal sphere model as a clinical tool.

The population of the study consisted of 37 patients referred by the Institute for Depth Psychology and Psychotherapy, the Psychiatric Hospital of the City of Vienna, and by several private practitioners. The sample represented a mixed group in terms of age and sex, and also in terms of diagnoses, which ranged from mild neurotic disturbances to severe chronic psychoses.*

In defining clinical validity—or clinical usefulness, as we also called it—we reasoned that the test would prove valid if it could confirm, correct, and possibly supplement the evaluations provided by the patients' physicians.

The study was divided into three independent phases: In the first phase, one of the examiners (K) tested the patients, and the other examiner (S) "blindly" scored the tests and wrote summary evaluations. In the second phase, which ran concurrent with the first, the clinicians evaluated their patients, or more correctly, committed their evaluations to writing. It is important to note this difference because of the variation in the relationships between patients and clinicians. Some clinicians knew their patients only briefly, others had treated them for years. In the third phase, the clinical evaluations and the test summaries were compared, and the clinicians rated the test according to fit and contribution in the following areas:

(1) Agreement between test and clinical picture; that is, is the patient clearly recognizable in the test?
(2) Does the test confirm the clinical evaluation?
(3) Does the test provide supplemental information, through correction, emphasis, or addition?
(4) Does the additional information influence the clinical diagnosis?
(5) Can new data from the test be clinically verified?

The ratings were given in five grades, from "very good" to "not at all."

The results for the first two categories were convincingly positive. The clinicians rated agreement and confirmation high, or at least clear, in all cases. In no case did they find that the test disagreed with their evaluation.

The results for the other three categories showed some variation: In two-thirds of the cases, the test was judged to provide useful additional information; in one-third it failed to do so, or the new information did not fit into the clinical picture. The ratings for diagnostic usefulness followed the same pattern. In the question of verification the sample was divided. The ratings, as such, were good: In 75% of the cases, new data from the tests could be verified in subsequent contact with the patients. However,

---

* The adaptation of the test for a non-American population was easily accomplished. It entailed only the translation of the routine instructions and of the terms used for the variables. A German language version of the personal sphere model has been published (Schmiedeck, 1973) and was used by Lyon in her work (Lyon, 1977).

the importance which these data assumed, and the degree of certainty with which they were verified, depended very much on the nature of the relationship between clinician and patient. In long-term, psychotherapeutic relationships, the data were rarely surprising, but judged to be meaningful in terms of confirmation, correction, and shifts in emphasis. In most of these cases, the patient was stimulated by the test and brought the new material into subsequent hours, where it could be explored and traced. In contacts with patients, which were brief and essentially evaluative, such opportunities were limited, and in consequence the clinicians felt more uncertain about new data.

Several other observations from this study are worth mentioning.

There was general consensus among the clinicians that the personal sphere model tends to focus on conflict and emphasizes psychopathology. It remained unclear whether this impression was caused by the test or by the bias of the examiner.

The models of the patients from the Psychiatric Hospital of the City of Vienna showed impoverished, unproductive designs. These patients were chronic, regressed psychotics, about whom we had little or no information. Their models reflected poverty in object relationships, but did not permit differentiations or conclusions about details. For example, we were unable to determine whether we were seeing a schizophrenic or an organic defect, or the results of heavy medication.

The division of the roles of test administrator and test interpreter made the evaluations more difficult, and less complete and certain. A good part of the personal sphere model; that is, the measurable variables, can be accurately scored without knowing the patient, but the opportunity to observe and follow him during the testing is of definite advantage in judging subtleties and rounding out the picture.

A very interesting study has recently been conducted by R. Sollod of New York University (Sollod, 1977). Sollod adapted the personal sphere model to group administration and used it to test a large sample of college students. His work is of particular importance because it presents the first large-scale attempt to extend the use of the personal sphere model to non-psychiatric subjects, explores the psychological validity of the variables, and points to potentials of the test that had not been conceived of originally.

Three aspects of Sollod's paper will be reviewed here in detail: the norms he was able to establish, the comparisons of personal sphere model scores with other meaningful criteria, and the solution of the total contribution of personal sphere model variables into independent factors.

The subjects of the study were 310 undergraduate students with a mean age of 18.8 years; of the sample, 145 were female and 165 were male.

The adapted version of the personal sphere model which Sollod used consisted of three 8½" × 11" mimeographed pages, prefaced by a face sheet which solicited demographic data. The first page contained the standard instructions for the test with minor variations. The second page was left blank except for the symbol of the "self" in the center. The last page inquired about the time needed to complete the personal sphere model and asked if any insights had been gained from it. Many subjects did not respond to the last page, and it was not used for quantitative analysis.

Administered in the same battery were a version of the Beck Depression Scale, a scale measuring Locus of Control (Rotter, 1966), and a Fear of Success Scale (Canavan-Grunpert et al., 1978; Pappo, 1972).

Sollod hypothesized that the number of family members in the tests would decrease with age and years in college, and that certain correlations would become apparent in the comparison of the personal sphere model with the other tests in the battery.

In the evaluation of the models, only objective characteristics were scored. The list of these characteristics included most of the basic PSM variables and a supplement of new variables and variations; for example: number of family (F); connections to family (Cf); crossbars relating to family (Crf); and a ratio of family to total objects (F/O). Table 8-1 summarizes the means for these categories.

The means in Table 8-1 are consistent with the means obtained in our investigation of psychiatric patients and in individual test administration. For example, Sollod found that the typical personal sphere model would consist of eight objects, seven of which are "people," and would have a bond index of 2.3 and a separation index of 0.4. The number of objects is small, but still within the expected range. As Sollod points out, it corresponds to subsphere #1, which is supposed to contain mainly family members. The values for the bond index and the separation index are equal to our means, including the somewhat higher mean for the bond index. By the standards of the clinical sample, Sollod's subjects were young; we also found higher bond indexes in adolescents.

In testing his assumptions, Sollod found that neither age nor class in school were significantly correlated with any of the PSM variables. This is not a surprising finding. Age could be expected to be correlated with the number of objects, but not within the small age range of a student population. He also found significant correlations between some indices on the personal sphere model and the Beck Depression Scale. Higher scores on the Beck scale corresponded to higher scores for the number of crossbars, the number of family crossbars, the separation index, and also to higher scores for the number of objects and the number of "people." No significant correlations were found between the PSM variables and either the Fear of Success or the Locus of Control scales.

Table 8-1

Means and Standard Deviations of PSM
Categories ($N = 310$)

Category	Mean	S.D.
Personal Sphere Model		
Basic scores		
1. Objects (O)	8.229	5.813
2. People (P)	6.835	4.818
3. Ideas (I)	0.468	0.997
4. Things (Th)	0.919	1.820
5. Connecting lines (C)	18.552	9.314
6. Crossbars (Cr)	3.781	6.523
7. Number of family members (F)	3.110	1.914
8. Family connections (Cf)	7.723	4.876
9. Crossbars—family (Crf)	1.045	2.728
10. Distance from center ($DCent$)[a]	22.310	9.070
Derived scores		
11. Proportion of family (F/O)	0.413	0.229
12. Proportion of family (Cf/C) connections	0.441	0.271
13. Proportion of family (Crf/Cr) crossbars	0.173	0.326
14. Proportion people (P/O)[b]	0.844	0.198
15. Proportion of ideas (I/O)[b]	0.055	0.114
16. Proportion of things (T/O)[b]	0.104	0.199
17. Bond index (C/O)	2.330	0.509
18. Separation index (Cr/C)	0.433	0.477

[a] This value is not directly comparable. Sollod measured distance in eighths of an inch to the furthest marking point.

[b] The corresponding values would be expressed in the object-ratio or the Idea %.

Since a comparison of PSM variables, selected from his list, yielded highly significant intercorrelations, Sollod decided to determine their individual contributions by subjecting them to a factor analysis. The seven factors that emerged were: productivity, family, ideas, things, interruptions, size of objects, and bonding. The most important loadings were: on *productivity* number of objects (0.96), number of "people" (0.95), and number of connecting lines (0.89); on *family* proportion family (0.86), family connections (0.86), and family members (0.85); on *ideas* number of "ideas" (0.96), and proportion of "ideas" (0.96); on *things* proportion of "things" (0.91), and number of "things" (0.80); on *interruptions* family crossbars (0.75), the separation index (0.68), and number of crossbars (0.62). Loaded on *size of objects* were size of objects (0.93), and differentiation of objects (0.70). Loaded on *bonding* was the bond index (0.72), and the number of connecting lines (0.39).

In terms of contribution to the total variance: productivity accounted for 23.8%, family for 19.1%, ideas for 11.3%, and things for 9.4%. The remaining three factors made smaller but still significant contributions.

In discussing the relationship between certain PSM variables and the Beck Depression score, Sollod speculated that depressive affect appeared to be related to the current experience of interruptions, which on the PSM is expressed in the total number of crossbars. For the subjects in Sollod's sample, largely college freshmen and sophomores, this experience of interruptions would seem to be linked to the transition from dependence on the family to independence.

Sollod showed that the personal sphere model can effectively be used in group administration, developed norms for a nonpsychiatric sample, and demonstrated the independence of various PSM characteristics. It is his conclusion that the test reflects, in part, the social world of the individual, and offers evidence of criterion validity. Sollod believes that the test is potentially useful not only in clinical application but also in personality research. He suggests as areas for further work the comparison of the models of defined subgroups and other concurrent validity studies, as well as the further elucidation of the meaning of PSM responses. Another area of suggested study is the relation between actual change in the social world of an individual (through death, separation, immigration, marriage, etc.) and the nature of the changes in the personal sphere model.

N. Lyon (Lyon, 1977) conducted a thorough and extensive study of the personal sphere model at the University of Graz in Austria, with the goal of objectifying and examining the reliability and validity of its data. She further hoped to improve the usefulness of the test as a clinical tool by refining and quantifying several of its variables.

In contrast to Sollod, who had used the personal sphere model in group administration, Lyon administered the test individually and was able to include the protocols and follow-up interviews in her evaluations.

The subjects of her sample were 100 undergraduate and graduate students from the Student Counseling Center of the University of Graz. This center is not a student mental health service in the usual sense, even though some students visit there because of minor emotional difficulties. Its primary purpose is guidance related to studies. The sample should therefore be considered a normal population.

The mean age of the subjects was 25.0 years; 45 subjects were male, 55 female; 20 were married, two divorced, 78 single; 12 had one child, four had two, and one had four children.

Each subject was given the PSM during his initial visit to the center; the retests were administered after intervals of one week and three months, respectively. Assignment to one or the other retest group was random. The first 50 subjects were assigned to group 1 (three months interval), the next 50 subjects to group 2 (one week interval). Both groups were comparable in terms of their demographic composition. Lyon obtained 86 retests, 43 in each group.

Reliability was determined through correlation of test and retest scores, validity through a comparison of the personal sphere model with the Multiple Attitude Test (Toman, 1955) and biographical data.*

Administration and evaluation of the personal sphere model followed the usual procedure, except that the subjects were systematically asked to explain their relationships, and to elucidate the nature of indicated interruptions. The demographic data obtained were: sex, age, marital status, number of children, number of members of original family, and professional or vocational training besides the present studies.

Lyon attempted to objectify and refine the categories of the PSM by adapting and subdividing several of the variables. She arrived eventually at a total of 42. Most interesting is her breakdown of interruptions. She differentiated six subcategories for the experience of separation *(Cr):* ambivalence, conflict–aggression, loss–mourning, distance, active, and passive. As has been mentioned, crossbars are indeed used to express a complex, and sometimes ambiguous set of feelings. Lyon's attempt to filter out the predominant emotion—or cause—seems worthwhile.

Important also is her classification of the mean distance. She established seven separate categories: the MD for family members, acquaintances and friends, sexual partners, male and female objects, people in general, and ideas.

Lyon further obtained the sequence in which objects were drawn, that is, whether people preceded ideas, male objects followed female objects, and the like. In addition, she noted (as we had done in our retest study) the objects which were found on tests as well as retests. She called these objects "identical objects."

Separate coefficients computed for the 42 variables in the comparison of tests and retests were significant on the 0.01 level, with the exception of

---

* The Multiple Attitude Test was originally constructed and standardized by W. Toman. It purports to provide a relatively large amount of information about a person, and its administration requires little effort from either tester or subject. The test is based on the successive sorting of various items and measures attitudes in twelve different realms. The attitudes used by Lyon for comparison with the PSM were: attitude toward parents; attitude toward siblings; preference for mother/father; preference for brother/sister; male/female prejudice; attitude toward children, toward superiors, and toward equals; religious tolerance; political tolerance; racial tolerance; attitude toward rich people. A separate quantitative score was computed for each of these realms.

only one. This particular coefficient was for the variable "Relative Re-
dundancy," which Lyon used but is not part of the standard set of the
test. The overall reliability coefficient derived by Lyon had the value of
0.649, and after applying the Fisher transformation for lower confidence
limits the value was 0.52. Both of these values are surprisingly high for a
projective instrument, and indicate that the personal sphere model measures reliably, on the whole and also on separate scores.

The respective overall coefficients for group 1—which was retested
after three months—were 0.65 and 0.46; and for group 2—retested after
one week—0.70 and 0.57. Since reliability coefficients tend to drop with
time, these results followed expectations.

Lyon also entertained the notion that scores which measure
"habitual" characteristics would show similar reliability coefficients after
one week *and* three months, while scores which measure "momentary"
characteristics (that is, moods, needs, feelings) would be subject to
greater fluctuation. On the basis of her results, she concluded that the
personal sphere model reliably measured both "habitual" and "momentary" characteristics.

Specifically, Lyon found the range of objects virtually unchanged
after either interval, and the scores for bonds, separations, distance, and
sequence of objects somewhat changed after three months. She reasoned
that the variable number of objects captures the relatively constant
"habitual" aspects of relationships, while the bond index, separation
index, mean distance, and mean difference in distance reflect more transient characteristics. Lyon thus arrived, independently, at results which
are very similar to the results of our retest study.

Validity was determined by correlating 43 PSM variables (the number
of identical objects was included at this point) with 12 variables of the
Multiple Attitude Test and four demographic items. The unique character
of the personal sphere model made it difficult to find an appropriate test
for comparison. The Multiple Attitude Test, which seemed to cover
related areas, was accepted as a "provisional criterion." In the factor
analysis, which followed the results of the correlations, 22 PSM variables
were used along with the 12 MAT scales and the four demographic data.
Nine factors emerged, of which each contributed at least 2.7% of the total
variance. Two of these factors showed substantial loadings only with
PSM scores, two other factors only with MAT and demographic data. The
factors loaded with PSM as well as MAT variables indicated that the
common aspects of the two tests were noteworthy but not especially large.
Lyon concluded that the personal sphere model and the Multiple Attitude
Test did not measure the same traits, but that their areas showed sufficient
overlap to regard the significant correlations as satisfactory.

This concluding statement is not surprising. One would have wished
for more definitive findings, but the nature of the personal sphere model

makes it indeed very difficult to find comparison criteria. I do not feel that this difficulty argues against the validity of the personal sphere model. The test covers aspects of the social world of the subject, of its interpersonal relationships, of emotional factors, and of cognitive elements. The variety of these data makes it probable that validation will have to be approached from several angles.

In her summary, Lyon states that the personal sphere model can best be used in the context of a test battery, or as a screening tool. For diagnostic use further validation is needed, for example, comparison with first-hand criteria such as ratings by clinicians, or application of the test in diagnostic extreme-groups. She feels that the personal sphere model offers meaningful and reliable information about the extent and the nature of interpersonal relationships, and suggests that the results should be interpreted on basis of psychoanalytic formulations, of role theory, and of concepts about human space.

At the conclusion of this chapter, I want to mention an ongoing study which introduces a new concept (Schmiedeck, 1977). In constructing a personal sphere model, a subject uses the basic variables (O,C,Cr) as building blocks. He sets them, as it were, and—with minor or major variations—develops his design. The succession in this process is cap-tured in the categories sequence and order. But while sequence and order refer to succession in time, there is also succession in space. As the subject places objects on the sheet, he establishes a pattern. For example, he may proceed very regularly, and follow the march of time around the clockface. He may move in a counterclockwise direction, or finish one sector and then reverse the trend and finish another sector. He may erect his model stepwise, one by one, or jump all over the place.

When one compares models from this vantage point, several separate factors become discernible. A model can be constructed in "steps," that is, small moves in space, one building on the other; or it can be con-structed in "leaps," movements over larger gaps. Most models seem to be built in a combination of steps and leaps. These progressions follow a "direction," and sometimes it seems that steps and leaps fall into a certain "rhythm"; for example, two steps and one leap, or several steps and several leaps.

It is too early to be sure, but it seems conceivable that we will find some typical progressions, and also some typical ways in which direction is pursued or changed. If this is the case, we might be able to obtain information about the way in which a subject goes about organizing space. (If, and to what degree, such sequences might follow cognitive patterns, is entirely speculative.)

REFERENCES

Canavan-Grunpert, D., Garner, K., & Grunpert, P. *The Success-Fearing Personality: Theory and Research.* Lexington, Mass.: Health, 1978 (in press).

Lyon, N. Die Objektivierung eines projektiven Testverfahrens: Das Modell der persoenlichen Sphaere. Unpublished doctoral dissertation, University of Graz, Austria, 1977.

Pappo, M. Fear of success: A theoretical analysis and the construction and validation of a measuring instrument. Unpublished doctoral dissertation, Columbia University, 1972.

Rotter, J. B. Generalized expectancies for internal versus external control of reinforcement. In *Psychological Monographs*, 1966, 80.

Schmiedeck, R. A. The Personal Sphere Model: General Data and Statistics. Unpublished manuscript, 1971.

Schmiedeck, R. A. Das "Personal Sphere Model," Versuch eines graphischen Tests fuer Objektbeziehungen. *Zeitschrift fuer Klinische Psychologie und Psychotherapie*, 1973, *21*, 164–82.

Schmiedeck, R. A. Steps in the construction of the Personal Sphere Model. Unpublished manuscript, 1977.

Schmiedeck, R. A. & Kohlmann, Th. Zur klinischen Validititaet des "Personal Sphere Models." *Zeitschrift fuer Klinische Psychologie und Psychotherapie,* 1975, *23*, 151–62.

Sollod, R. The Personal Sphere Model: Norms, psychometric properties, and concurrent validity in a college population. Unpublished manuscript, Dept. of Psychology, New York University, 1977.

Toman, W. Multiple Attitude Test. *Journal of Abnormal and Social Psychology,* 1955, *51*, 163–70.

9
Theoretical Considerations

The personal sphere model contains a variety of data from different realms. The attempt to understand and trace these data will therefore have to move in several directions.

The model provides information about interpersonal relationships, and to the extent that this information is translatable into dynamic terms, it could be called a map of libidinal attachments. However, the test also offers insights into the nature of ideas, and allows us to measure emotional conditions. In short, it seems to convey the kind of information which, under different circumstances, we elicit in interviews. Thus, one might think of the test as a kind of interview, in which responses are given graphically rather than verbally, or graphically and verbally. The graphic aspect opens an avenue which is less under conscious control than verbal statements, and in addition provides data on spatial and cognitive elements.

Occasionally, one finds a subject who develops the model as if it were his personal story accompanied by illustrations. Such models are usually intriguing and offer a great deal of information.

There are several tests that appear to be similar in function, concept, or appearance, and need to be differentiated from the personal sphere model. My intention here is not to review all tests that could possibly have some connection or resemblance, but only those which can be considered to have substantial similarities.

The "World Test," originally introduced by Loewenfeld (1939) and further developed by Buehler et al. (1951), has been used primarily with children. It uses play as a medium for obtaining information about family relationships, attachments, fantasies, and conflicts. The interpretation focuses on the presenting problem and the general orientation toward the surrounding world.

Kelly's (1955) "Role Repertory Test" is based on his theory of social constructs. It employs a verbal method to identify the degree of intimacy between a subject and significant figures in his environment, and to gauge the extent to which these figures have influenced attitudes and conflicts in the subject's life. A limitation of this test, as Kelly himself points out, lies in the use of the verbal approach.

Ziller et al. (1964) developed the "Self-Social Orientation Tasks," which are based on Kelly's concept of social constructs and list of significant figures. Ziller attempted to overcome the limitations of the verbal approach by devising a visual system in which objects represented by circles are arranged in predetermined topological configurations. For example, a horizontal line of several objects represents a left-to-right hierarchy, and the relative placement of the self (that is, the circle representing the self) within this serial order is used as a measure of self-esteem; a triangle of three significant others is formed by the examiner, and location of the self within rather than without this "social triangle" is presumed to be related to social interest (Ziller et al., 1968, 1969; Ziller, 1969). Ziller is mostly interested in social adaptation and uses concepts such as self-esteem, self-interest, identification, and self-centrality as the crucial components in the orientation of the self to others.

Both Kelly's Role Repertory and Ziller's Self-Social Orientation Tasks are conceptualized within the framework of social psychology. They do not extend their range of application to dynamic formulations. Also, their structures are imposed upon the subjects to a larger degree than in the personal sphere model, and projection is not part of the test concept. Ziller's Self-Social Orientation Tasks may show some superficial similarity in appearance, but they serve a different goal and are not constructions or designs that the subject develops.

More closely related to the personal sphere model in conceptualization are the sociograms, originally introduced by Moreno (1973). They are diagrams reflecting relationships between the members of a group, and use graphic means to express the nature of these relationships. Women are represented by circles, men by triangles. Feelings for individuals are expressed as lines between these symbols; for example, full lines for positive feelings, broken lines for negative feelings. The intensity of emotional response is indicated in numbers ..., 1, 2, 3,... placed next to the lines. These designations represent preferences—choices between different members of the group, rather than feelings with historical roots; and the diagrams refer to given situations—the interactions of a limited number of people rather than to the total sphere of relationships of an individual. Most importantly, the sociograms are not tests or models developed by the subject, but diagrams produced by an observer.

In the sociometric perception test (Leutz, 1974), which builds on the theory of the sociograms, this has been changed. It is now up to the subject himself to indicate his relationships in sociometric terms. For this test, a differentiation is also made between an inner nucleus of real attachments, the so-called social atom, and an outer range of wished-for relationships. This concept is clearly related to the notion of distance in the personal sphere model. In fact, it comes about as close to the idea of a personal sphere as any concept we have found. It is, however, not identical. In the sociometric perception test, interpersonal relationships are also looked at from a social point of view and in a given situation within a group, and the notations are prescribed, offer limited freedom for elaboration, and do not contain elements of projection or of spatial and cognitive representations.

The Semantic Differential, developed by Osgood and his associates (1971) and used frequently and widely, may appear to be similar to the personal sphere model. Osgood is interested in the meanings that significant persons, ideas, or situations have for the individual. The approach is essentially a combination of controlled association and rating scales. While stimuli from several modalities—visual, auditory, emotional, and verbal—may share in the significance, their meanings are funneled only verbally, through the associations. In other words, the test taps verbal thought. Meaning is allocated "positions" on scales between bipolar adjectives (e.g., good–bad, beautiful–ugly, and long–short). These positions, when followed through a set of interrelated scales, form a "direction" or "dimension" along which meaning varies. Given several such dimensions, and several concepts that have a place somewhere on these dimensions, distances between the concepts become measurable.

Osgood arrives at a three-dimensional model by visualizing these dimensions interacting orthogonally. The point at the center of this space is 0, and meaning extends from there along the directions.

At a later stage, Osgood constructs such space models by using sticks of different length and rubber balls. The apparent similarity to the personal sphere model is eyecatching. Also, the concept of distance, as Osgood uses it, reminds one of the concept of distance in the sociometric perception test, and is being used to measure affective charges—or better, affective differentials.

Probably one need no longer emphasize this point. A number of approaches use spatial distance to indicate emotional meaning. Another example can be found, not in a test, but in the concepts of human space and human territory described by Hall (1959, 1966). The common source lies in the interrelationship of feeling and distance, which is self-evident and part of our daily language.

Osgood describes three studies in which the semantic differential was used to measure the meaning or ways of perceiving significant persons and situations. In all three, the sophistication of the test instrument was not matched by the level of clinical assessment. Yet, there are some obviously interesting and valuable findings. Changes in psychotherapy are reflected in shifts in the measured distances; ambivalence and conflict find expression in difficulties in the judgment process, which is in turn reflected in positions close to the center on the bipolar scales. The most intriguing study is that of a case of triple personality (pp. 258–271), in which the shift from one personality to the other is visualized in different semantic space models. In these figures, the authors (Thigpen & Cleckley, 1954) find that good is up and bad is down, active is to the left and passive to the right, strong away from the viewer and weak toward the viewer. This finding has obvious bearing for the location of affect in space. Unfortunately, the model seems to have been constructed by the authors, and therefore it is not clear whether the directions are artificial or correspond to intrinsic concepts of the patient.

The correlations between affective meaning and location in space become clearer in several experiments conducted by Pecjak (1972). His paper has been mentioned earlier, in the context of discussing the placement of "significant people." Pecjak used a graphic form of the semantic differential. He asked his subjects to respond to affectively charged key words (e.g., friend–enemy, goodness–evil, joy–sadness) by assigning them a location on a sheet of paper, and evaluated these locations according to a division of space along certain dimensions. The most important dimensions were: above–below, along a horizontal division; left–right, along a vertical division; center–periphery, related to distance; and foreground-background, related to depth. Pecjak's division of space is interesting and important for the placement of objects on the personal sphere model. However, it is not clear from his paper whether he accounted for the possibility of base distributions.

There might be still other tests that relate to the personal sphere model in one way or another. An example would be the Giessen Test (1975), which Lyon originally considered for use in her correlations. It is based on psychoanalytic concepts, and employs a verbal method for obtaining information about a subject and his relationships. Judging from our difficulties in procuring a good comparison instrument, it seems unlikely that any of these tests would come close enough to the personal sphere model to warrant delineation.

To summarize, the main features which seem to set the personal sphere model apart are:

1. The model is a construction of the subject.
2. The guidance and/or interference of the examiner is limited and leaves ample room for individual variation and expression—including projection.
3. It is possible to arrive at inferences about cognitive and spatial aspects.
4. The main elements of the test are nonverbal, but verbal expression is not excluded.
5. The variables, except for the basic three *(O, C, Cr)* are not givens, but are derived from an analysis of many models, and only secondarily reintroduced.

The original concept of the personal sphere model was based on two ideas: The notion of a personal sphere, and the use of graphic notations for the representation of interpersonal relationships *(O, C, Cr)*. When we applied this model, the results began to show certain regularities and groupings, and properties emerged which we have since learned to recognize and categorize. However, there remains the question of what these properties mean, and what a personal sphere model actually is: Is it a map of interpersonal relationships? A collection of object images? Does it reflect personal space, affective loading, the boundaries of the body image, or a cognitive sphere? Or does it contain all of these elements?

The following considerations are an attempt to look at these questions from several vantage points. They follow a certain order, but are not necessarily complete or systematic.

ASPECTS OF DRAWING

Most obviously, the personal sphere model is a graphic representation, a drawing. As such, the aspects of drawing which are clinically meaningful should apply. Lerner (1972) developed a projective instrument in which the subject copies the designs of the Bender Gestalt. She believes that through the process of "seeing" (the patterns of the Bender), clusters of associations are stimulated, and that the subject projects attitudes, wishes, and anxieties into his reproductions. The drawings are evaluated in terms of general style, size, consistency, roundedness vs angularity, sloppiness vs orderliness, fragmentation asf. On basis of these features, inferences can be made—particularly in serial drawings—about the subject's life style, and his coping and defense mechanisms. Essential for Lerner is the manner in which the subject approaches the task and organizes the material.

DiLeo (1970) also emphasizes the need of paying attention to how a subject draws, and only secondarily to what he draws. To DiLeo, graphic movements are a kind of kinesthetic activity, and like bodily movements are influenced by emotional and intellectual factors.* Developmentally, DiLeo places the transition of motoric movement patterns to representational drawings between the ages of three and four. He says that by ten years of age most non-artistic people have reached their highest level of drawing ability, on which they will no longer improve. This fact may well account for the rather primitive drawings we see in many personal sphere models. DiLeo reports several other relevant observations. The first figure drawn by children, other than vertical or horizontal lines, is a circle; and a circle also becomes the first representation of the human body, especially the head. I have assumed that circles are used in personal sphere models because they copy the sphere of the "self." It is possible that their choice might also be based on this early form of representing the human figure.

Later in the development of drawing, extremities are added to the circle, and eventually another circle for the trunk. When the latter circle is replaced by a line, we have a stick figure. Sex differences are first indicated by long hair for females, and only much later by trousers or skirts. All these features are often found in personal sphere models. We have, in fact, used them to gauge the degree of differentiation, which was graded from "labels only" over "circles" to "stick figures" to fully drawn "faces and figures."

BODY IMAGE AND BODY IMAGE BOUNDARIES

Drawings have also been used in the study of body image and body image boundaries.

Kotkov and Goodman (1953) found that obese women draw figures that cover an unusually large area of paper. Wysocki and Whitney (1965) showed that the figure drawings of crippled children had significantly more "areas of insult" than those of normal children. Kamano (1960) examined a sample of schizophrenic women and arrived at significant correlations between ratings for the concept My Actual Self on the

---

* The connection of kinesthetic activity and drawing becomes also clear in Sollod's finding of a significant correlation between depressive affect and a high number of crossbars (see pp. 40 and 171). Sollod assumes that it is the very act of drawing, the motoric emphasis, which expresses the feeling.

Semantic Differential and ratings for like-sex figure drawings. Simmons (1966) compared figure drawings of college students with their self-evaluations by means of the Semantic Differential and adjective check lists, and also found significant correlations between ratings for the Actual Self and ratings for like-sex drawings.

From these studies, it appears that correlations exist between the perception of the body image and its reflection in figure drawings. Fisher (1972), from whose book these examples are taken, discusses the validity of this proposition, and cites several investigations in which it was critically examined. I will follow his exposition, since the conclusions, even though based on figure drawings, seem to have bearing on the drawings in personal sphere models as well.

Levi, (1961), who investigated a group of disabled subjects, attempted to answer the question of a direct relationship between the body image and the drawn figure. She felt that such an "isomorphic relation" had to be proved before one could attribute overemphasis in the drawings to a preoccupation of the subject with the injured part. Levi's sample consisted of subjects with arm or leg disabilities, low back disabilities of poorly defined etiology, and a group of normals. She found that individuals whose bodies are disabled are indeed particularly sensitive to the perception of the injured region in representations of the human figure, but only if the disability takes a clearly visible form.

Apfeldorf (1953) examined the connection between figure drawings and the projection of the "bodily self" in a matching experiment. He obtained figure drawings from two groups of college students: (1) those with a normal amount of body interest, and (2) physical education majors who were assumed to have an unusually high body investment. The figure drawings were matched with full-length photographs of the subjects. The results proved significant for the first group. In a follow-up experiment, in which frontal drawings of the female figure were matched with photographs, Apfeldorf and Smith (1965) again obtained matchings which were significantly higher than chance. The data supported the proposition that elements of the subjects' self-concepts were projected into their sketches.

Fisher (1972) concludes the like-sex figure drawings produced by an individual mirror aspects of his feelings about his body, and also, to some degree, attitudes toward himself as a person. "Body type, age, physical appearance, and body anxiety do seem, in many cases, to find representation in the individual's drawings (p. 72)."

The following examples do not refer to drawings per se, but still deal with the projection of the body image and its perception in forms that permit clinical evaluation.

Schafer (1960) found a "fragmentation" of the body image in the Rorschach tests of schizophrenics. Their protocols showed body percepts which "split, inflate, get crushed or crippled, die, or get lost in each other or in undefined and topsy-turvy space."

Roth and Blatt (1974a & 1974b) examined Rorschach protocols for signs of "transparency." They posit the existence of spatial representations in the mind, which correspond to developmental levels. Insufficient differentiation between the self and the object is reflected in "transparent" responses, indicating, as it were, unclear boundaries and confusion of developmental layers. Examples of "transparency" are responses in which objects are seen through glass or water, or which refer to the porosity or permeability of fabrics and surfaces. Roth and Blatt feel that their findings apply to the state of the body—as well as the ego boundaries.

Closer in design to the personal sphere model are studies by Hozier and by Horowitz. Hozier (1959) studied a group of schizophrenic women and a normal control group to ascertain whether there would be differences in body image integration and in the perception of the body's spatial position. Three types of tasks were used:

1. The subject was asked to place male and female cutout figures into picture scenes.
2. A model doll had to be reproduced from an array of thirty different doll parts.
3. A "whole person" had to be drawn.

The results indicated that the schizophrenic subjects had greater difficulty than the normals in all three tasks. Hozier interpreted her findings to mean that schizophrenics suffer from a "diminution of narcissistic cathexis of the body" which results in a breakdown of the bodily self and a disturbance in space perception.

Horowitz et al. (1964) showed that schizophrenics have larger "body-buffer zones" than normals. They measured the size of these zones in terms of how closely a subject approached various objects and persons, and in terms of the boundaries which the subjects drew around the figure of a person in order to indicate a comfortable distance. Schizophrenic patients consistently maintained a greater distance between themselves and others.

The authors reasoned that the space adjacent to one's body should be regarded as an integral part of the body image, and that schizophrenics require a larger intervening space because of the vulnerability of their body image boundaries.

In a later experiment, Horowitz (1967) used drawings of visual impressions in situations which tend to lower reassurance from the environment: when falling asleep or waking up, while looking at bright spaces, and while closing one's eyes. He found that the visual imagery emerging from these experiences contained information which is not carried into consciousness by word representations.

Rose (1966) conceived of body boundary disturbances as anchored in poorly developed object relationships. He felt that many symptom patterns are maneuvers designed to bolster weakly defined boundaries, and mentioned as examples the head-knocking and self-biting of autistic children.

On basis of these and other studies, Fisher (1972) arrived at the conclusion that attitudes about one's body are often the result and reflection of interpersonal relationships. He suggests that the body image boundary is conceptualized as an interiorized system which varies relative to the nature of the relationships that were the prototype for the system: "If an individual's interactions with the mother figure have been such that she had a series of meaningful, clear-cut, and stable expectations from him and he in turn developed similar patterns of expectations of her, one would assume that the interiorized system growing out of the relationship would have definite, well articulated boundaries (p. 309)."

The studies reviewed above support the notion that the personal sphere model, in addition to information on object relationships and affective content, also conveys information on the state of body image and body image boundaries.

IMAGE REPRESENTATION

Krohn and Mayman (1974) believe that the individual's capacity for object relationships depends greatly on his repertoire of object images, and that the level of object representation appears to be a salient and consistent personality dimension, which expresses itself through "a diverse set of psychological avenues... from dreams to psychotherapy." According to Knapp (1969), inner images are directly translated into outer expressions, and can be found in emotional display, pantomime, or the "endless variety of art forms." It is likely that the graphic representations of the personal sphere model belong to these outer expressions, and the question of their translation from inner images is very pertinent. However, before we approach this question, we should look at the way in which the personal sphere model permits images to pass into representations; that is, we should look at the control the variables exert over data.

The variables connecting lines and crossbars, and consequently the bond index and separation index, tap the affective charge in relationships.

They show relatively frequent intra-individual changes and are, more than any other variable, under conscious control. The instructions define their use and range, and it must be assumed that the subject remains aware of these directions. That this conscious awareness is not complete is demonstrated in cases where crossbars are omitted or added in unusual numbers, or where connecting lines are left out. At any rate, though, the affective charge of relationships appears to be the most superficial layer tapped by the test, and reflects meaning which is close to awareness.

In contrast, the variables mean distance, mean difference in distance, Vollgestalt, and Praegnanz show little intra-individual change, and appear to be largely removed from conscious control. All these variables have to do with the Gestalt of the design. There is nothing in the instructions that would regulate them or draw attention to their being part of the test. They tap a deeper layer, it seems, and may be related to cognitive styles, concepts of personal space, and body image boundaries.

The third group of variables, the number of objects and the percentage of ideas, appears to lie between the two groups mentioned. For the percentage of ideas one would assume some degree of conscious control. However, it seems to be small. The percentage of ideas indicates the presence of or preoccupation with issues, which are considered part of the self. The retest study showed considerable intra-individual change in this area, more often an increase in ideas. This increase remained well within the usual range, however, and did not reach dimensions which would have pointed to a withdrawal from relationships. It may reflect a slightly greater awareness of the self and its contents.

The number of objects remained very consistent from test to retest. The means did not change at all, and the standard deviations showed only negligible fluctuations. Such consistency cannot be explained by a total absence of change. In fact, this is not what it meant. Subjects did change objects. They dropped grandparents or former lovers, and added friends or therapists. But it was always an exchange, in terms of composition, and not a change in terms of numbers.

The instructions do not regulate the number of objects, as is evident from the great variation in ranges (from 6 to 43). In other words, there are substantial differences in the size of the object range, but once an individual has chosen his range he stays with it. Therefore, it seems that the range of objects is determined by factors which are not readily conscious, and may represent the influence of deeper layers. In discussing this question, I would like to concentrate on "people." The average subject appears to think of about twelve "people" with whom he has, or has had, important relationships ($Q1-Q3 = 8-18$). We found that the number of "people" is correlated with age. Young subjects have a smaller range, older subjects a wider range. But this finding has no influence on the cluster around twelve, and does not help to explain it. Why is the average not eight or 20? One wonders if twelve is the number of people we can comfortably "handle." We might feel overwhelmed by more, and impoverished with fewer. Experiences in group work seem to point in this direction. But we may have stumbled upon a basic characteristic in the organization of human relationships. Calhoun (1966) investigated the living habits of small mammals, and thinks that his findings have important implications for the understanding of the formation of human groups. These small mammals, mice and shrews, gather their food in a circular area, called the "home range." If the "home range" is subdivided into three concentric circles, one finds that the outermost circle is visited least often, and the innermost circle most often. To utilize resources fully, individual "home ranges" overlap with their outer circles, forming "constellations." Usually a "constellation" includes twelve individuals and their "home ranges." "This number (of 12), applies to a host of species, as divergent as the Norway rat, howler monkeys, or man in his more primitive state." Calhoun concludes that evolution, in developing the most effective use of resources, will normally favor species living in compact groups of about twelve, and that man has long been related and adjusted to this group size because it offers the most harmonious way of life.

In summary, the personal sphere model seems to consist of elements which are more or less consciously controlled. The more controlled variables are likely to express structured connections and verbal thought, the less controlled variables are apt to permit passage of visual imagery, cognitive aspects, and preconscious and unconscious content.

I return now to the discussion of image representation.

Sandler and Rosenblatt (1962) speak of the development of representations in language which is strikingly similar to the language of the personal sphere model. According to the authors, the child creates a representational world by gradually forming stable images. This world contains objects and things, body representations, and need and affect representations. It is necessary to differentiate between images, which are detailed temporary representations, and representations per se, which are larger, more permanent schemes.

With the establishment of object representation there emerges self-representation. Ego boundaries are formed. Finally, the representational world may be compared to a radar or television screen providing meaningful information upon which action is based. The ego makes use of self, object, or affect representations, and of the symbols derived from them.

Another way of looking at image representation is suggested by Rapaport (1967), who distinguishes two kinds of cognitive structures: (1)

quasi-permanent means which cognitive processes use and do not have to recreate each time, and (2) quasi-permanent organizations of such means that are the framework for cognitive processes.

Cognitive processes are temporary and unique; their organizations are permanent and typical. The organizations are responsible for cognitive styles: styles of personal memory, or of the representational organization of object relationships.

As one progresses from waking to hypnagogic to dream thought, verbalization decreases and visual imagery becomes increasingly predominant. We can distinguish stages of cognition by objective criteria, which are not qualitative but quantitative parameters. Some of these criteria are: visual imagery, verbalization, explicitness vs. implicitness, and differentiation or elaboration. Also, we know that visual memory images contain many of the spatial, temporal, and personal relationships that are cognized through them.

Speculating along these lines of thinking, one could say that the personal sphere model sets up a motivational intent to tap visual image memory, in particular spatial, affective, and personal aspects of relationships. These aspects are reproduced within the framework prescribed. What emerges are memories and their structural organization, that is, cognitive or libidinal maps characteristic of the individual. One could further say that the subject moves along two frames of reference in developing his model: a subjective-psychological frame of reference leading to visual, pictorial presentations with affective coloring; and a perceptual frame of reference which adheres to the instructions and contains verbal, formal, and schematic elements.

Knapp (1969) approaches the same question by a different route. In speaking of the translations of inner images into outer expressions, he says that in planning and searching "we scan inner maps . . .from which we select and articulate . . .details . . .the images in these maps represent aspects of the world in some degree of abstraction and schematization." They are mental representations along a spectrum from the literal to the predominantly abstract, and to a varying degree serve a symbolic function. Following Langer (1951), Knapp distinguishes discursive and nondiscursive symbolisms. Discursive symbolisms, such as words or mathematical notations, are relatively neutral and precise, and have generally agreed upon meanings and rules of combination. They correspond to secondary process thinking. Nondiscursive symbolisms are presentational, ambiguous, idiosyncratic, and personal. As a mode of mental activity they precede discursive language. They present information simultaneously and their informational value derives from their organization or spatial patterning. Imagery, for the most part, takes place in the nondiscursive form.

Horowitz agrees with Knapp. In the paper already mentioned (1967), he states that the imagery, which emerges in place of word representation, in particular the pictorial imagery, belongs to an earlier, developmentally more primitive cognitive system, which has its own utility as the carrier of charged memories and ideas. Possibly, it might also have its own characteristic pattern of circuitry or physiological substrate. In a later paper, Horowitz (1972) elaborates further. He now differentiates between three separable systems through which information is processed: enactive, image, and lexical representations. Enactive representations are concrete and contain memory of motor action. Lexical representations are abstract and essentially word representations. Image representations are intermediate between these two. The most common variety of image representation are visual images, which are excellent in conveying information about the form and spatial relationship of objects, and which often, with or without instruction, reveal previously repressed memories and fantasies.

Horowitz explains that for him the term "representation" is not limited to unconscious aspects of information, but reflects an organization of information that can be part of conscious experience. As information is processed, it is built into organizational schemata which develop into schematic representations of self, object, world, and inter-object activity. Visual images develop "spatial-simultaneous formats" which organize the information about the spatial and temporal contiguity of objects and their constancies, similarities, and differences. In a still later paper, Horowitz (1975) introduces the concept of enoptic images. These are images which can be traced to stimulation within the optic system itself, the physiological substrate. They are simple hallucinatory or pseudo-hallucinatory experiences, such as circular figures, radiations, parallel lines, or amorphous specks or blobs. They form a matrix upon which images from higher centers build. Under the impact of certain motivational states they can be uninhibited, impinge upon the representations from higher centers, undergo secondary elaboration, and find their way into conscious image experience. Depending on the extent of discontrol this results in illusions, hypnagogic experiences, or hallucinations.

Using Knapp's and Horowitz's formulations, I can now repeat the attempt of suggesting a rationale for the translation of images into the representations of the personal sphere model.

It could be that the visual symbol of the "self," in combination with the instructions, sets up a motivational state which taps visual image memory. Indeed, the test, by insisting on pictorial representation, compels the subject to translate lexical thought into visual imagery—backwards, as it were. This imagery is not allowed to roam freely. It is, at least in part, constricted to a given number of variables which force a mode of expression on the subject, albeit not a rigid mode.

We could also say that the instructions and basic variables represent discursive, abstract symbolisms, and are used to organize the nondiscursive, presentational symbolisms of the visual imagery. They are the tools, the building blocks, so to speak, while the architecture comes from deeper, less defined layers of memory and cognition. Through the structure of the variables, some of the richness and fluidity of visual imagery is lost. On the other hand, this very structure enables us to decipher and retranslate the pictorial representations into verbal thought.

REPRESENTATION OF SPACE

It remains to discuss the representation of space in personal sphere models. We have assumed that one can draw conclusions from the manner in which this space is organized, and from the way in which distance is being used. Such an assumption implies that the spatial relationships on the personal sphere model reflect mental representations, which in turn reflect the conditions of actual relationships and the style in which these relationships are organized.

The meaning of distance seems to be self-evident and intuitively understood. It is also fairly well documented. Hall (1966) divides space into four different distances: intimate, personal, social, and public. He gives the actual distance in feet for each, and describes the sensory involvement, which lessens as the interval increases. He further specifies that the distance chosen depends on the nature of the transaction and the relationship between the interacting individuals.

Little (1965) and Little et al. (1968) performed a series of experiments in which he had line drawings of human figures arranged according to their relationship. He found significant increases in distance between the figures depending on whether they were seen as friends, acquaintances, or strangers. He also found that the two figures were placed closer when they were thought to share beliefs and values.

Kuethe (1962 & 1964) showed that the sense of "belongingness" is related to grouping and distance. He placed two objects at a given distance, removed them, and had his subjects reconstruct the setting. In a succession of experiments he could prove that the reconstruction distance deviated from the original according to the kind of relationship the objects were supposed to have. For example, two male figures facing away from each other were replaced at a distance greater than the original; two rectangles were replaced at the original distance; and two men facing one another were replaced at a closer distance. Kuethe used these experiments to demonstrate that grouping and distance are incorporated in "social schematas," and that these schematas are strong enough to lead to errors in judgment. In a second set of experiments he explored the dependence of social schematas on specific stimuli, and found that their influence was pervasive whether the stimulus was presented verbally, visually, or in some other form.

Somewhat related are the sensori-tonic experiments by Glick (1964), who could show that objects acquire different qualities when they are felt to be related to one's body. The perceptual quality of objects—for example, their apparent spatial position—alters as soon as an individual shifts from seeing them as "out there" to seeing them as related to his own body.

This phenomenon has bearing for the placement of objects in the personal sphere model. We know, for example, that children tend to be placed into the right half, between two and five o'clock, and that women are inclined to put children closer to the "self."

It appears that we can distinguish two types of distance in personal sphere models:

1. the distance to individual objects, which carries affective loading, and is closely related to valence (the ratio Cr/C). As has been mentioned, the degree of emotional involvement is expressed in either distance or valence—or both—and there may be individual preferences for the one or the other mode.
2. the "total" distance of a sphere, scored in the variables MD and MDD. This distance appears to be related to style, to the characteristic or "habitual" way of spacing relationships. To some degree it may also be related to Horowitz's "body-buffer zone."

Certain aspects of the organization of space in personal sphere models are difficult to define. They have to do with the total impression of the Gestalt, and with the distribution of objects, their density, clustering, and distance from the "self," and with the overall sense of balance and harmony. These aspects are remindful of Jung's archetypes (Jung, 1968)—for example, the sunwheel, which shows four or eight partitions, or his model of the mental sphere which places sensation and thinking farthest out, and affects closest to the center.

Looked at in this way, the personal sphere would represent the self, with the actual "self" as a core. Looked at in another way, the model would encompass a larger space, in which the "self" represents the self and the body, and the surrounding space the human territory. It seems to make little sense to be pedantic in this differentiation. Probably the representations shift back and forth between a narrower and a wider concept. But the notion of the surrounding human territory has interesting connotations.

According to Proshansky et al. (1970), the human territory is the physical space surrounding the person, and is an essential means of establishing and maintaining a sense of identity. Proshansky says that individuals define a space for themselves in order to reduce pain and discomfort, and that this space is closely related to a feeling of privacy and freedom of choice. There are individual states of privacy, such as solitude and anonymity, and group states of privacy, such as intimacy and reserve, which need consensus. In either case, these states are related to the available distance and territory, and individuals differ greatly in their spatial needs.

Stea (1965) discusses the properties of physical space. The space in which people live is defined physically and through behavior. Human territories can be stationary or moving, individual (human territory in the strict sense), or collective (shared territories, in clusters or complexes). Space has properties such as shape, size, a number of units, extensiveness, types of boundaries, differentiation in detail, relatedness, asf. There is obvious similarity between these concepts and the concepts of the personal sphere model, even though Stea speaks of physical and not emotional space. Stea even mentions that the human interaction within these territories can be sketched, and that it must be assumed that people possess a mental map of their individual space and of the shared clusters.

It is helpful to consider the development of spatial concepts. Beck (1970) has done this in a paper on the meaning of space. He distinguishes three basic kinds: objective space, which is the space of physics and mathematics; ego space, which is the individual's adaptation of observed space; and immanent space, which is the inner, subjective space of the unconscious. Immanent space includes the spatial styles and characteristic orientation and reference systems, which are the result of prolonged and complex exchanges between the individual and his environment, and derive from all three kinds of space. Beck uses five parameters to describe these styles and systems: diffuse vs dense space, delineated vs open space, verticality vs horizontality, right and left in the horizontal plane, and up and down in the vertical plane.* He found that in young children, up to the age of six, these parameters are fused into a single system. In the next five years, gradual differentiation occurs into left–right, up–down, and horizontal–vertical. By the age of thirteen, all five parameters are included and space has become fully differentiated and meaningful. Individual differences in the differentiation of space depend on age, sex, and profession; more importantly, they appear to reflect the development of object relations and the sense of the self as distinct from others.

In concluding, I shall return once more to the influence of representational schemes on the personal sphere model, even if this may entail some repetition.

---

* The relation to Pecjak's classification of space is obvious (p. 182).

In his review article on cognitive theory, Scheerer (1954) traces a number of concepts that seem closely related to elements of the personal sphere, and might help us explain how these elements are constructed. According to Tolman (1932), cognition is defined as "the initial orientation towards a goal-object in terms of distance, direction, and valence character . . .and as the selection of a means-object or path in terms of its suitability for reaching the goal. Cognition is an intervening variable 'mediating' between the stimulus situation and the resultant behavior act."

The complex "object–distance–direction–valence" in the personal sphere model could, in this sense, be termed a cognitive unit, or a unit carrying cognitive meaning.

Bateson (1951) says that there has to be a translation of external events into internal events (and vice versa), a substitution of one type of event for another. This translation takes place through codification. For information to be useful, the relationship between the internal and the external must be systematic, and therefore it is possible to have internal objects or events so related to each other that their relations reflect relationships between parts of the external.

If the notations of the personal sphere model are related to an internal code, as we think they are, they would reflect a part of the internal cognitive system.

Gibson (1950) distinguishes between the "literal visual world" and the "schematic visual world," which is a centrally mediated representation. The schematic view is synonymous with cognitive structuring, and consists of abstractions and meanings which the individual imposes upon his literal perceptions.

Self and object are part of the same cognitive field. The self is an ever-present anchor point. Only under particular circumstances, such as early developmental stages or border states, does the representational field lose this dual reference of self and non-self.

Several experimental studies established a bridge between cognition and emotion. Michotte (1950) performed experiments using simple geometric figures, such as two-colored rectangles, which moved towards and away from each other, under varying conditions of speed, direction, and distance. These movements and the changing positions of the rectangles were experienced as "joining," "getting together," "flight," "fear," "separation," asf. Michotte felt that specific sequences of motion were thus perceived as causally related "felt connections."

Heider and Simmel (1944) had their subjects observe a movie, which presented different geometric figures; for example, a small triangle, a large triangle, a circle, and a rectangle, in varying combinations and movement sequences. The subjects described the figures not only as human, but in terms of interpersonal relationships such as rivalries or conflicts. Heider concluded that the relations of temporal succession, spatial proximity, and continuity, are decisive conditions for the causal and interpersonal perceptions involved.

For these experiments it would seem that motion is in part—or even primarily—responsible for the experience of emotion in the observer. Yet, motion does not appear to be an essential ingredient.

Otnow and Prelinger (1962) describe a test of the capacity for intimacy, in which they use abstract designs to tap emotional response. They invented new and unfamiliar nonobjective drawings, and established that these drawings evoked feelings about closeness, competence, stability, love, sex, anger, and so forth. These drawings were static, and only through their very nature and their pairing did they elicit emotion (and a feeling of movement).

The personal sphere model also conveys a feeling of motion. We speak of objects being held closely, or moving away, of expansive designs, of fluctuations of distance, etc; or we note the absence of motion in such designations as rigid, bland, and mechanical. It is conceivable that the experience of motion, and thus emotion, enters through the successive steps in the construction of the design and the very acts of drawing, which are retraced by the observer.

The thoughts expressed in this last chapter reflect my own present understanding of the personal sphere model, and my attempts to find explanatory and supporting evidence. Even though this book is mainly written as a manual I hope that some of them will arouse interest and stimulate further thought and research.

REFERENCES

Apfeldorf, M. The projection of the body self in a task calling for creative activity. Unpublished doctoral dissertation, University of North Carolina, 1953.

Apfeldorf, M. & Smith, J. The representation of the body self in human figure drawings. Unpublished paper presented at the annual meeting of the Eastern Psychological Association, Atlantic City, New Jersey, 1965.

Bateson, G. Information and codification: A philosophical approach. In Ruesch, J. & Bateson, G. (eds), *Communication: The Social Matrix of Psychiatry.* New York, Norton, 1951, pp. 168–211.

Beck, R. Spatial meaning and the properties of the environment. In Proshansky, H. M. (ed), *Environmental Psychology: Man and His Physical Setting.* New York, Holt, Rinehart & Winston, 1970, pp. 134–41.

Beckmann, D. & Richter, H. E. *Giessen-Test: Ein Test fuer Individual und Gruppendiagnostik.* Bern–Stuttgart–Wien: Hans Huber Verlag, 1975.

Buehler, Ch., Kelly Lumry, G., & Carrol, H. S. World-test standardization studies. *Journal of Child Psychiatry*, 1951, *2*, 2–81.

Calhoun, J. B. The role of space in animal sociology. *Journal of Social Issues*, 1966, *22*, 45–58.

DiLeo, J. H. *Young Children and Their Drawings*. New York, Bruner/Mazel, 1970.

Fisher, S. *Body Experience in Fantasy and Behavior*. New York: Appleton–Century–Crofts, 1972.

Gibson, J. J. *The Perception of the Visual World*. Boston: Houghton Mifflin, 1950.

Glick, J. A. An experimental analysis of subject–object relationships in perception. Unpublished doctoral dissertation. Clark University, 1964.

Hall, E. T. *The Hidden Dimension*. Garden City, New York: Doubleday, 1966.

Hall, E. T. *The Silent Language*. Garden City, New York: Doubleday, 1959.

Heider, F. & Simmel, M. A study of apparent behavior. *American Journal of Psychology*, 1944, *57*, 243–59.

Horowitz, M. J. A cognitive model of hallucinations. *American Journal of Psychiatry*, 1975, *132*, 789–95.

Horowitz, M. J. Modes of representation in thought. *Journal of the American Psychoanalytic Association*, 1972, *20*, 793–819.

Horowitz, M. J. Visual imagery and cognitive organization. *American Journal of Psychiatry*, 1967, *123*, 938–46.

Horowitz, M. J., Duff, D. F. & Stratton, L. O. Personal space and the body-buffer zone. *Archives of General Psychiatry*, 1964, *11*, 651–56.

Hozier, A. On the breakdown of the sense of reality: A study of spatial perception in schizophrenia. *Journal of Consulting Psychology*, 1959, *23*, 185–94.

Jung, C. G. *Analytical Psychology, Its Theory and Practice*. New York: Pantheon, 1968.

Kamano, D. K. An investigation of the meaning of human figure drawing. *Journal of Clinical Psychology*, 1960, *16*, 429–30.

Kelly, G. A. *The Psychology of Personal Constructs*. New York: Norton, 1955.

Knapp, P. Image, symbol and person. *Archives of General Psychiatry*, 1969, *21*, 392–406.

Kotkov, B. & Goodman, M. Prediction of trait ranks from Draw-a-Person measurements of obese and non-obese women. *Journal of Clinical Psychol.*, 1953, *9*, 365–67.

Krohn, A. & Mayman, M. Object representation in dreams and projective tests. *Bulletin of the Menninger Clinic*, 1974, *38*, 445–66.

Kuethe, J. L. Pervasive influence of social schemata. *Journal of Abnormal and Social Psychology*, 1964, *68*, 248–54.

Kuethe, J. L. Social schemas and the reconstruction of social object displays from memory. *Journal of Abnormal and Social Psychology*, 1962, *65*, 71–74.

Langer, S. K. *Philosophy In A New Key*. New York: Mentor, 1951.

Lerner, E. A. *The Protective Use of the Bender Gestalt*. Springfield, Illinois: Charles C. Thomas, 1972.

Leutz, G. *Psychodrama: Theorie und Praxis. Das klassische Psychodrama nach J. L. Moreno*. Berlin: Springer Verlag, 1974.

Levi, A. Orthopedic disability as a factor in human-figure perception. *Journal of Consulting Psychology,* 1961, *25,* 253–56.

Little, K. B. Personal space. *Journal of Experimental and Social Psychology,* 1965, *1,* 237–47.

Little, K. B., Ulehla, J. Z. & Henderson, Ch. Value congruence and interaction distances. *Journal of Social Psychology,* 1968, *75,* 249–53.

Loewenfeld, M. The world pictures of children: A method of recording and studying them. *British Journal of Medical Psychology,* 1939, 18, 65–101.

Michotte, A. The emotions regarded as functional connections. In Reymert, M. I. (ed), *Feelings and Emotions.* New York, McGraw–Hill, 1950, pp. 114–26.

Moreno, J. L. *Gruppenpsychotherapie und Psychodrama.* Stuttgart: Georg Thieme Verlag, 1973.

Osgood, Ch. E., Suci, G. J., & Tannenbaum, P. H. *The Measurement of Meaning.* Urbana, Illinois: University of Illinois Press, 1971.

Otnow, D. & Prelinger, E. An abstract design test of the capacity for intimacy. *Perceptual and Motor Skills,* 1962, *15,* 647–54.

Pecjak, V. Affective symbolism of spatial forms in two cultures. *International Journal of Psychology,* 1972, *7(4),* 257–66.

Proshansky, H. M., Ittelson, W. H. & Rivlin, L. G. Freedom of choice and behavior in a physical setting. In Proshansky, H. M. (ed), *Environmental Psychology: Man and His Physical Setting.* New York: Holt, Rinehart & Winston, 1970, pp. 173–83.

Rapaport, D. Cognitive structures. In Gill, M. M. (ed), *The Collected Papers of David Rapaport.* New York: Basic, 1967, pp. 631–664.

Rose, G. Body ego and reality. *International Journal of Psychoanalysis,* 1966, *47,* 502–09.

Roth, D. & Blatt, S. J. Spatial representation and psychopathology. *Journal of the American Psychoanalytic Association,* 1974b, *22,* 854–72.

Roth, D. & Blatt, S. J. Spatial representations of transparency and the suicide potential. *International Journal of Psychoanalysis,* 1974a, *55,* 287–93.

Sandler, J. & Rosenblatt, B. The concept of the representational world. *Psychoanalytic Study of the Child,* 1962, *17,* 128–45.

Schafer, R. Bodies in schizophrenic Rorschach responses. *Journal of Projective Techniques,* 1960, *24,* 267–81.

Scheerer, M. Cognitive theory. In Gardner Lindzey (ed), *Handbook of Social Psychology.* Cambridge, Massachusetts: Addison–Wesley, 1954, pp. 91–142.

Simmons, A. D. A test of the body image hypothesis in human figure drawings. Unpublished doctoral dissertation, University of Texas, 1966.

Stea, D. Space, territory and human movement. *Landscape,* 1965, *15,* 13–16.

Thigpen, C. H. & Cleckley, H. A case of multiple personality. *Journal of Abnormal and Social Psychology,* 1954, *49,* 135–51.

Tolman, E. C. *Purposive Behavior in Animals and Men.* New York: Century, 1932.

Wysocky, B. A. & Whitney, E. Body image of crippled children as seen in Draw-a-Person test behavior. *Perceptual and Motor Skills,* 1965, *21,* 499–504.

Ziller, R. C. The alienation syndrome: a triadic pattern of self-other orientation. *Sociometry*, 1969, *32*, 287–300.

Ziller, R. C., Hagey, J., Smith, M. D. C., & Long, B. H. Self-esteem: A self-social construct. *Journal of Consulting and Clinical Psychology*, 1969, *33*, 84–95.

Ziller, R. C., Megas, J., & DeCencio, D. Self-social constructs of normals and acute neuropsychiatric patients. *Journal of Consulting Psychology*, 1964, *28*, 59–63.

Ziller, R. C., Long, B. H., Ramana, K. V., & Reddy, V. E. Self–other orientations of Indian and American adolescents. *Journal of Personality*, 1968, *36*, 315–30.